IT TOOK A CRISIS

May this book enable you to unpack
our past, give you hope in the present,
and challenge you to radically
transform for a more equitable
future.

[signature]

10.05.21

IT TOOK
A CRISIS

HOW A PANDEMIC MADE SOCIAL
DISRUPTION GO VIRAL

JORDAN JOHNSON

NEW DEGREE PRESS

IT TOOK A CRISIS
How a Pandemic Made Social Disruption Go Viral

ISBN   978-1-63676-760-4   *Paperback*

978-1-63676-761-1   *Kindle Ebook*

978-1-63676-762-8   *Ebook*

CONTENTS

INTRODUCTION

———

It was 9:00 p.m. on a Monday in September when it hit me. I could feel it brewing in my chest.

To quell the anxiety, I needed to focus on something—anything. I replied to e-mails from work; then opened an Excel spreadsheet, determined to deal with the project I had put off for weeks.

My heart palpitated.

That's it! That's what's making me anxious, I told myself. *This feeling will go away, if I can just get this formula to work in my model.*

COVID-19 had turned our apartment—like most homes across the country—into our workplace.

I bellied up to the kitchen table I called a desk, took a huge swig of Cab Sav, and focused my eyes and thoughts on the grid before me. An hour later I had balanced the numbers in my financial model. I also had tears streaming down my face.

Across the room my fiancé looked up from his laptop, noticed my emotional state, and rushed to my side.

"Is everything okay? Is everyone in your family safe? Did something happen at work?"

He posed the questions one might ask someone who has erupted into tears—to which I replied in blubbering and incoherent half sentences.

"Everything is just so fucking bleak," I said.

The feeling in my chest that night wasn't anxiety but weight. The weight of a global pandemic, of quarantine, and of confinement. The weight of the recession and of an election. The weight of climate change. The weight of intersectional oppression and of being a Black woman in corporate America. The weight of cell phone video making me an eyewitness to the murder of unarmed Black and Brown people—over and over again. The weight of calling my family to confirm it wasn't us this time. The weight of thanking God it wasn't us this time—not this time.

I couldn't process the magnitude of these crises unraveling around me. I found strength in the realization that I was not alone in my paralyzing fear, and then I found purpose.

So began my author's journey: my calling to bear the tide of the COVID-19 pandemic, document the disproportionate outcomes of this crisis, and share my perspective on where we go next.

Joe Biden got it right in his speech before the Democratic National Convention in August 2020. The man who would become the forty-sixth president of the United States described the four concurrent crises gripping the nation and, in many ways, the world:

> *The worst pandemic in over 100 years. The worst economic crisis since the Great Depression. The most compelling call for racial justice since the 60s. And the undeniable realities and accelerating threats of climate change. (Pramuk, 2019)*

These outcomes are not isolated events. When deficient health care infrastructure and global isolationism fail to contain a contagion, the disease can spread across borders and leap over oceans. When a government fails to provide individuals and small businesses with adequate safety nets, the fiscal impact of a pandemic can spiral into an economic crisis. Injustice thrives when those in power uphold oppressive institutions, policies, and systems. Where skeptics deny the existence of man-made climate change its perilous impact cannot be slowed or reversed.

No single systemic failure arose because of a crisis. Instead, each crisis magnified and exposed cracks that were already there. Like parts in an assembly line, one crisis informs the next. When we acknowledge the interdependencies among these issues, we can design meaningful solutions to correct systemic inequity.

Take the United States' public health response to COVID-19 for example.

The Centers for Disease Control and Prevention (CDC) Foundation defines public health as the science of protecting and improving the health of people and their communities, accomplished "by promoting healthy lifestyles, researching disease and injury prevention, and detecting, preventing and responding to infectious diseases."

Seems pretty critical, right? You would think. However, according to the Centers for Medicare & Medicaid Services' public record on health care expenditures, the United States spends just 3 percent of the nation's $3.8 trillion health care budget on public health activities. By contrast, 73 percent of the budget is reserved for health care insurance, including Medicare, private health insurance, Medicaid, and other federally funded insurance programs.

Due to the rapid advances in medicine that took place in the twentieth century—from eradicating polio and smallpox to the development of antibiotics—"[by] the end of the twentieth century, public-health improvements meant that Americans were living an average of thirty years longer than they were at the start of it." (Yong, 2020) This is exactly what public health is meant to do. However, these improved health outcomes were not rewarded with continued funding, and they became a target for budget cuts instead. Essentially our government took an "If it's not broke, don't fix it" stance on public health investment.

With this mind-set, the federal government began pulling funding for public health. Between the late 1960s and the 2010s "the federal share of total health expenditure for public health dropped from 45 percent to 15 percent. As a result, states were required to cover the gap in funding mostly on their own." (Haseltine, 2020) Naturally this resulted in regional disparities, as not all states are equipped with the resources to address this gap.

To make matters worse, between 2003 and 2019 the CDC cut funding for state and local public health emergency preparedness and response by a third. (McKillop et al, 2019) Without this funding these institutions did not have the resources required to manage public health under normal circumstances, let alone a global pandemic.

One estimate—as researched by Nason Maani, public health expert, and Sandro Galea, dean of Boston University School of Public Health—suggests that United States' public health departments are currently $4.5 billion short in funding to "provide a minimum standard of foundational public health capabilities." The wording here is extremely important. We are $4.5 billion short of providing the *minimum* standard in this country.

More shocking is the fact that the United States spends nearly twice as much as the average OECD country on health care. (Tikkanen et al, 2020) The OECD, or Organisation for Economic Co-operation and Development, was founded in 1961 to stimulate economic progress and world trade and has thirty-eight Member countries to date.

Despite this high spending compared to peers, however, the United States has some of the worst health outcomes, as summarized by Roosa Tikkanen and Melinda Abrams in their brief "U.S. Health Care from a Global Perspective,

2019: Higher Spending, Worse Outcomes?" Compared to the average OECD country, we have the lowest life expectancy and highest suicide rates. Adults have the highest chronic disease burden. We have the highest rate of obesity. We visit the doctor less frequently and have fewer physicians.

And this is before these numbers are even segmented by race.

How could this be? Our per capita health spending is the highest in the world, but this spending does not translate to improved health outcomes. A team of researchers at the Johns Hopkins Bloomberg School of Public Health found that "higher overall health care spending in the U.S. was due mainly to higher prices—including higher drug prices, higher salaries for doctors and nurses, higher hospital administration costs, and higher prices for many medical services."

Our pre-COVID-19 health care infrastructure could barely manage the day-to-day demands of our ongoing crises—including obesity, opioid addiction, and contaminated water systems.

Funding for community prevention, public health emergency preparedness, and chronic disease prevention programs declined, while the number of emergencies increased. In fact, in 2017 alone there were "eighteen declared public health emergencies [...] compared to twenty-nine combined declared emergencies for the prior ten years." (McKillop et al, 2019)

This trend indicates that as the threat of crisis grew our health care infrastructure shrank, hindering our ability to adequately prepare and respond when things went south. It took a global pandemic to get government officials to pay attention to these pleas for prevention.

The COVID-19 outbreak catalyzed a perfect storm for our fractured, underfunded public health system:

- Underinvestment in emergency preparedness and response infrastructure left us vulnerable to a pandemic. And negligent national leadership hindered acute attempts to contain the virus.
- Failure to address systemic risk factors contributing to high rates of chronic diseases resulted in a collision of chronic disease, systemic inequality, and a viral outbreak—magnifying the burden of the pandemic for vulnerable populations.
- Hasty roll out of stay-at-home advisories did not account for individuals whose jobs could not be performed remotely. The resulting spike in unemployment left millions of families without health care or a safety net.
- Essential workers—who are more likely to be Black, make a household income of less than $40,000, and not hold a college degree—are forced to work on the front lines of the crisis. (Kearney et al, 2020)

Twelve months after researchers in Washington state confirmed the first case of the novel coronavirus on our shores COVID-19 had killed more than 350,000 Americans. (Harcourt et al, 2020)

This tragedy forced us to take stock of the status quo, to rationalize how we got here. Turns out when people start questioning the status quo, some pretty amazing changes can happen.

In 2020 alone there were many changes catalyzed because of—not in spite of—the pandemic:

- More Americans voted in the November 2020 election than in the past 120 years, with nearly every state hitting a new record turnout. (Schaul et al, 2020)
- The protests this summer were "the largest movement in the country's history, according to interviews with scholars and crowd-counting experts." (Buchanan et al, 2020) Polling suggests that fifteen to twenty-six million Americans participated in demonstrations over the murder of George Floyd and other Black and Brown people at the hands of law enforcement.
- Adoption of digital technologies has been accelerated by several years. According to a survey of 899 C-level executives their organizations have "accelerated the digitization of their customer and supply-chain interactions [...] by three to four years. And the share of digital or digitally enabled products in their portfolios has accelerated by a shocking seven years." (LaBerge et al, 2020)
- American pharmaceutical giant Pfizer broke a record for the fastest go-to-market vaccine in history after receiving approval from the United Kingdom public health authorities to distribute the COVID-19 vaccine for widespread commercial use. (Georgiou, 2020)

The COVID-19 health crisis has catalyzed a series of events that will likely change the course of history for years, perhaps decades, to come—in my opinion, for the better.

***

One of my favorite quotes is from the movie *Enemy*, a neo-noir psychological thriller mystery starring Jake Gyllenhaal. The plot takes many twists and turns—*admittedly, I was still a bit confused even at the end*—but the opening was profoundly simple and simply profound. No Hollywood magic. Just a black screen with clean, white text and these five words: "Chaos is order yet undeciphered." (Villeneuve, 2013) I couldn't think of a better summary for why I have written this book.

I wrote this book to decipher the chaos of the coronavirus pandemic. To lay bare the existing institutional failures that our nation has failed to address for decades—arguably centuries. These issues are not new. Health care has never been a universal right in the United States. Science has always been political. People of color have been unjustly murdered at the hands of law enforcement for centuries. What *is* new is the public discourse and open dialogue that this crisis has inspired.

I ask, against this backdrop, if we should ever go back to normal? Normal never quite served us.

This crisis has unlocked a powerful force, equipping us—as global citizens—to reimagine a more equitable reality.

In the following chapters I share how this crisis has transformed—and in many cases accelerated—social justice initiatives, public health reform, private and public sector innovation, consumer shopping behaviors, and other aspects of our sociopolitical life. I acknowledge that these shifts in public consciousness did not happen in a vacuum and explain these events as part of a broader historic and cultural context we must understand to truly engage in a meaningful conversation on current events. Lastly I share my perspective on what this should mean for our future and how we might effectuate meaningful change by understanding the dynamics of disruption during times of crisis.

"Not everything that is faced can be changed," wrote James Baldwin, "but nothing can be changed until it is faced." (Baldwin, 1962)

If you see this crisis as a time for transformation this book will provide you with the language and knowledge to responsibly tap into these pockets of opportunity.

If you see this crisis as a tragedy, perhaps this book will give you hope.

PART I

THE CRISIS

CHAPTER 1

DON'T FALL OFF
THE CLIFF

———

Imagine there was a gigantic cliff right next to your neighborhood.

Despite coordinated efforts by your community representatives cautioning people to avoid the cliff, every day it seems you hear a new story about one of your neighbors falling off the edge.

Thanks to the ambulances waiting at the bottom these individuals have all made full recoveries. You wonder what could have been done to prevent this tragedy in the first place.

A safety net might catch individuals before they hit the ground, but some may fall through the holes. You consider starting a petition for the city to install a trampoline halfway down the cliff but you know some individuals won't be able to bounce their way back up to the top. You contemplate a fence building campaign but doubt a fence could be built strong enough to withstand the wear and tear of such a large population.

After contemplating these scenarios, you realize your community's safest option is to move away from the cliff entirely.

***

In a lecture on public health Dr. Camara Jones—a renowned American physician, epidemiologist, and antiracism activist—uses this analogy to illustrate the role public health should play within our communities. Each strategy represents a health intervention.

The ambulance at the bottom of the cliff is tertiary prevention, which "[prevents] the complications from a disease that's already manifested." (DocFleaPhD, 2017) In this example the EMTs treat the injuries associated with falling from the cliff.

The net, trampoline, and fence represent secondary prevention—safety net programs such as early screening and detection initiatives. These interventions have the potential to save individuals as they are falling off the cliff but do not address the fact that large portions of the population are at risk of coming close to the edge.

Shifting the community away from the cliff describes primary prevention dedicated to addressing the social determinants of health. These determinants are "beyond our genes, they're beyond our individual behaviors and they are in fact the context in which our behaviors arise and in which they can confer either risk or protection." (DocFleaPhD, 2017)

They shape our access to food, education, health care, transportation, and safety. They inform our environment and influence our ability to thrive.

The coronavirus pandemic proved how critical public health is to our emergency response strategy and highlighted the dire consequences associated with underinvesting in this infrastructure.

One study suggests that developing a nationwide public health infrastructure would require funneling an estimated $4.5 billion of additional funding into the public health system. (McKillop et al, 2019) This funding would allow public health agencies, such as the Centers for Disease Control and Prevention, to invest in comprehensive health initiatives, address critical risk factors, and provide evidence-based interventions to promote positive health care outcomes. (McKillop et al, 2019)

It would require approximately $4.5 billion to develop a *foundational level* of public health infrastructure across the country. Referring to Dr. Jones's "cliff of good health" analogy, this means we have a very weak fence—that is only getting weaker—protecting us from falling off the cliff.

A 2019 annual report issued by the Trust for America's Health (TFAH)—a nonpartisan, nonprofit health policy organization—examines public health funding trends at the federal, state, and local levels and provides a series of investment and policy recommendations on how the country might prioritize prevention to effectively address current public health threats.

Their forward-looking recommendations center around three core initiatives: community prevention programs, chronic disease prevention, and public health emergency preparedness and response.

Community prevention programs seek to address the underlying conditions that contribute to an individual's or community's health. Studies show determinants such as the local economy, education level, public safety, access to quality education, economic opportunity, transportation, and housing are all elements that contribute to an individual's well-being and life expectancy.

These programs are designed to address the social determinants of health, which account for about 80 percent of health outcomes, by improving the environmental conditions that can lead to chronic disease, substance abuse, and other negative externalities. (McKillop et al, 2019)

Community prevention strategies boast substantial returns on investment. For example, "school-based violence prevention efforts can achieve a return ranging from $22 to $66 for every $1 spent and tobacco control mass media campaigns have demonstrated returns ranging from $7 to $74 per $1 spent." (McKillop et al, 2019) These strategies not only take a holistic approach to managing health care outcomes but also can often be extremely cost-effective. The TFAH concluded funding for these programs was inadequate as access to these programs is not available nationwide.

Programs like the CDC's State Physical Activity and Nutrition (SPAN) initiative—which focuses its efforts on improving nutrition, encouraging physical activity, breastfeeding, and food service guidelines—only had enough funding to implement programs in sixteen states.

In other cases, funds may be rerouted from one vital program to benefit another. This is what happened to the Racial and Ethnic Approaches to Community Health (REACH) initiative—a program deploying evidence-based, community level strategies to eliminate racial and ethnic health disparities in chronic disease and related risk factors.

Since 2017 "REACH grantees experienced a $53 million diversion in funds to the Good Health and Wellness in Indian Country program, which supports effective community-chosen and culturally adapted strategies to reduce the leading causes of chronic conditions, increase health literacy, and strengthen community-clinical links." (McKillop et al, 2019) In this case community programs are suffering from internal cannibalization as funding decisions for one program may result in the diversion of funds from another.

With these deficits in mind the TFAH recommended increasing funding of the SPAN program—by an additional $40.8 million in 2020—to expand the program to all states and adequately address the obesity crisis. They also suggest allocating an additional $21 million in funding to the REACH program while still ensuring there is adequate budget to fund the Good Health and Wellness in Indian Country program.

In fiscal year 2019, 11 percent of the CDC's budget—approximately $804.5 million—was allocated for funding of the Prevention and Public Health Fund (PPHF), the first dedicated source of federal funding for prevention and public health. (McKillop et al, 2019) The fund's intended use was to "improve health and help restrain the rate of growth in private and public sector health care costs." (McKillop et al, 2019) With this mission, the fund was successful in making investments in evidence-based programs by expanding vaccine infrastructure, building laboratory and surveillance capacity, and promoting tobacco cessation.

Against its authorized purpose, however, the PPHF has been used to fund health care services rather than promote preventative interventions.

The Affordable Care Act is a prime example.

With a renewed focus on prevention the Affordable Care Act planned to increase public health funding by $15 billion under the PPHF; however, a 2012 law cut this funding by $6.25 billion to fund Medicare physician fee cuts. (Maani et al, 2020) Sequestration, the process whereby the federal government makes automatic budget cuts for certain government programs, led to "a 5 percent cut to the overall CDC budget, a $160 million budget reduction for local, county, and state public health assistance, $25 million less for global infectious disease programs (including the Strategic National Stockpile), and $13 million less for emerging infectious diseases." (Maani et al, 2020)

The 2017 Tax Cuts and Jobs Act reduced the PPHF by $750 million to cover the costs of the Children's Health Insurance Program. (Maani et al, 2020) Each program merits additional funding, while this myopic financing strategy raises costs and worsens health outcomes in the long run by impeding prevention tactics.

This creates a negative feedback cycle whereby prevention efforts that could mitigate negative health outcomes are defunded to directly treat these negative externalities. Stated succinctly in the report, "treatment should not be funded at the expense of prevention." (McKillop et al, 2019) Combatting this appropriation of funds would require a longer-term funding strategy that protects the Prevention Fund by ensuring the reserve is used for its designated purpose.

The TFAH specifically recommended increasing funding to $824 million for the CDC's Public Health Emergency Preparedness (PHEP) cooperative agreement program in fiscal year 2020—the main source of federal support for state and local public health emergency preparedness and response—"to ensure states and localities have the core resources needed to respond to an escalating number of emergencies." (McKillop et al, 2019)

These emergencies are particularly acute due to limited funding for community prevention programs as well as a lack of investment in PPHF-sponsored chronic disease prevention and health promotion programs.

The CDC defines a chronic disease as a condition that "last[s] 1 year or more and require[s] ongoing medical attention or limit[s] activities of daily living or both." (Centers for Disease Control and Prevention) Chronic diseases such as asthma, diabetes, and heart disease—to name a few—are the leading cause of death and disability in this country. (McKillop et al, 2019) Sadly, 40 percent of adults in the United States have two or more chronic diseases and 90 percent of annual health care expenditures are for people with chronic and mental health conditions. (McKillop et al, 2019)

Funding cannot stop here. Needs for additional preparedness programs under the Assistant Secretary for Preparedness and Response—such as the Hospital Preparedness Program (HPP)—must also be addressed.

The HPP provides every state and territory with funding and technical assistance used to prepare their health systems for sudden disasters, support research and development, and stockpile medical countermeasures as necessary. (McKillop et al, 2019) Over the past sixteen years funding for this program has been nearly cut in half, consequently placing our hospital systems at severe risk should an outbreak emerge. The TFAH estimated that an additional $474 million would address this funding deficit. (McKillop et al, 2019)

Investment in our nation's emergency preparedness is critical to ensure we are able to respond timely to a major health crisis.

Funding trends across community prevention programs, chronic disease prevention, and public health emergency preparedness highlight how woefully unprepared we were as a country to manage the demands of a global pandemic.

Community prevention efforts were severely hampered by the absence of a national strategy for slowing the spread of the virus. The federal government failed to implement top-down stay-at-home orders, mask mandates, economic reopening plans, and school shutdown/reopening guidelines.

This limited coordination led to a highly fragmented public health response which ultimately resulted in an estimated $16 trillion loss—approximately 90 percent of the United States' annual gross domestic product—due to reduced economic output. (Cutler et al, 2020)

Public health preparedness and response faltered on three critical fronts: international partnerships, national leadership, and public health governance. From an international perspective President Donald Trump left the United States seat on the executive board of the World Health Organization (WHO) empty for more than two years, he pulled more than thirty staffers out of the CDC's office in China, and in July of 2019 he defunded an American epidemiologist embedded within China's CDC. (Yong, 2020)

Withdrawing from these critical international partnerships—aligned with President Trump's "America First" campaign rhetoric—hampered our nation's knowledge of the virus as well as our response agility. We lost the one thing we could not afford to lose: time.

We could not carefully study the virus before it reached our border. We did not work with our international peers to extract lessons learned from their response strategies to optimize our emergency response. We did not mass-produce tests to detect the virus or stockpile protective equipment.

As the United States reported its first case of COVID-19 our president claimed, "We have it totally under control. It's one person coming in from China. It's going to be just fine." (Neilson et al, 2020) This couldn't have been further from the truth.

In 2018 President Trump disbanded the White House pandemic response team, the very team that would have prepared for and supported a response to this pandemic. As if that wasn't enough, "American intelligence agencies warned about the coronavirus threat in January, but Trump habitually [disregarded] intelligence briefings. [Similarly] the secretary of health and human services, Alex Azar, offered counsel and was twice ignored." (Yong, 2020) President Trump failed to use his full authority to properly respond to the virus.

While public health is typically regulated at the state level, as outlined by the Tenth Amendment, in the case of a state of emergency the President "may use the Public Health Service (PHS) to such an extent and manner that in their judgment promotes the public interest." (Haseltine, 2020) By employing these powers the president would have had the ability to override state public health authority and drive a coordinated national response to the pandemic.

In the absence of such a strategy, state responses to the pandemic exacerbated preexisting resource disparities and contributed to a fractured public health response across the nation. This splintered response was reinforced by a lack of national public health governance.

Public health organizations have done their part to provide science-based guidelines and timely health information in response to the crisis but they lack the authority to hold states accountable for adhering to their recommendations.

The Federal Emergency Management Agency (FEMA) and the Public Health Service (PHS) both have "constitutional and legislative right to lead our national response to COVID-19," however, deficient executive leadership has limited their ability to hold states accountable for public health outcomes. (Haseltine, 2020) The negligence of our nation's leadership certainly hampered acute attempts to contain the virus, but the low prioritization and underinvestment in our emergency preparedness and response infrastructure made us vulnerable to such a crisis in the first place.

The nation's failure to address the systemic risk factors contributing to high rates of chronic diseases also came to a head due to the coronavirus outbreak. As the findings from a Global Burden of Disease Study indicate, "several of the risk factors and non-communicable diseases (NCDs) highlighted by the study, including obesity, diabetes, and cardiovascular disease, are associated with increased risk of serious illness and death from COVID-19." (Newsroom, 2020)

The intersection of chronic disease, systemic inequality, and COVID-19 magnifies the burden of the disease for vulnerable populations. The study describes the convergence of these three phenomena as syndemic—referring to the interaction of multiple epidemics. "The syndemic nature of the threat we face demands that we not only treat each affliction, but also urgently address the underlying social inequalities that shape them—poverty, housing, education, and race—which are all powerful determinants of health," the editor-in-chief of the *Lancet Medical Journal* explained. (Newsroom, 2020)

Our marginalized populations are also the most likely to be exposed to and contract the virus.

At the onset of the virus many states issued stay-at-home advisories requiring that individuals stay at their place of residence except for permitted work, local shopping, or other authorized errands. For some individuals these orders prompted their employers to establish programs for remote work, while for many others this translated to unemployment or dangerous working conditions.

As a result of these safety precautions unemployment rose to 14.7 percent, "the highest level since record-keeping began in 1948. More than twenty-six million people lost their jobs, a catastrophe in a country that—uniquely and absurdly—ties health care to employment." (Yong, 2020) The inextricable tie between access to health care and employment opportunities left millions of citizens without insurance at a time when they needed it the most. For many of these individuals the threat of prohibitively high out-of-pocket health care expenses resulted in avoiding the health care system altogether.

Individuals whose jobs have been categorized as "permitted work," thus excluding them from state stay-at-home ordinances, are forced to work on the front lines of the crisis to survive. These fifty million Americans often referred to as "essential workers" are made up of individuals supporting health care services, emergency services, grocery and convenience stores, restaurant carry-out, fast food operations, farms, manufacturing, transportation services, and more.

Studies show that these essential workers are more likely to be Black, have a household income of less than $40,000, and not hold a college degree. (Kearney et al, 2020)

Essential workers are already more likely to live in lower--income households, and they are now more financially insecure due to the economic impacts of the pandemic. The same poll found that "essential workers report having more difficulty affording necessities, such as credit card bills, utilities, and food, and are also more likely to say they are 'very worried' or 'somewhat worried' about affording food specifically because of the crisis." (Kearney et al, 2020)

The lack of structural support provided to unemployed and low-income individuals in the early stages of the crisis disproportionately impacts marginalized communities at the intersection of race, ethnicity, gender, citizenship, and socioeconomic status.

The outcomes faced by marginalized communities are shaped by the accumulated disadvantages—embedded and deeply intertwined—in our systems and institutions. These outcomes highlight the need to develop multidisciplinary and multidimensional responses to crises in order to enact meaningful change at the intersection of health care, public policy, and community development.

Take recent hazard pay legislation, for example. Typically associated with jobs such as those in the military service or mining, hazard pay is defined as supplementary pay for performing work considered hazardous or involving physical hardship. (Kinder et al, 2020) At the start of the pandemic it seemed the definition of a hazardous work environment needed to expand to address the needs of the fifty million essential workers risking their lives to provide critical services to their communities.

In April 2020 the House of Representatives passed legislation "to create a $200 billion hazard pay fund, while dozens of large companies were offering small, temporary hourly pay bumps and bonuses to frontline workers" (Kinder et al, 2020). Hopes were high that a federal hazard pay fund may alleviate the financial burden of the crisis, but these attempts ultimately failed due to lack of support from the Senate.

In the absence of a national response, many states have taken the initiative to create innovative hazard pay programs to address the needs of their marginalized communities. Pennsylvania's COVID-19 PA Hazard Pay Grant Program stands out as a particularly equitable model.

By October of 2020 the fund provided more than forty thousand frontline workers with the equivalent of a ten--week three-dollars-per-hour raise. Even with a $50 million program the fund only addressed the needs of 10 percent of applicants. (Kinder et al, 2020) As a result, officials "applied a strong equity lens to focus the limited funds on the greatest need." (Kinder et al, 2020) Applicants with the lowest income, highest risk of COVID-19 transmission, and minimal opportunities for federal support programs were given priority. Additionally, eligibility was limited to workers who earned less than twenty dollars an hour working in essential industries as defined by the state.

We can only imagine the impact a program like this might have had for essential workers if it was rolled out at the federal level.

Hazard pay is just one example of how the government may address the disproportionate burden of the pandemic on low-income people of color. The lack of institutional support provided to these marginalized groups highlights the systemic racism that perpetuates these structural gaps and underpins the negative health and financial outcomes of these communities.

"We cannot treat our way out of these problems. We are never going to build enough medical services. Preventing suffering before it happens is the long-term answer for our country. Our goal is to create a community where everybody has the opportunity to thrive," stated the director of the Center for Innovation in Pediatric Practice at Nationwide Children's Hospital in Columbus, Ohio, as she accepted the Hearst Health Prize for population health. (Raths, 2020)

To create this community our country must take a hard look in the mirror. We must come to terms with our nation's history of oppression, perpetuated by capitalism, and develop solutions designed for communities by communities. We must remove the barriers that keep our citizens from thriving so that one day we will not be so close to the edge of this cliff.

CHAPTER 2

VIRUS HUNTERS

B814 was an elusive virus. For years Dr. David Tyrrell had struggled to cultivate the sample, but virus B814 resisted. Dr. Tyrrell—the former head of the Common Cold Research Unit in Salisbury—was completely stumped. When he heard about the new viral imaging methods being piloted at St Thomas' Hospital in London, he took his chances and sent the sample there. "We were not too hopeful but felt it was worth a try," he wrote in his book *Cold Wars: The Fight Against the Common Cold*. (bioMérieux Connection, 2020)

Luckily for him the sample landed in the hands of June Almeida. Almeida had studied Immune Electron Microscopy (IEM) extensively. (Marks, 2020) Her peers affectionately called her "green fingers" because of her natural gift for using this method to visualize viral particles under the microscope. (Marks, 2020) Almeida carefully studied the B814 collection. Her IEM imagery brought into focus "viral particles [displaying] short spiky projections on their outer surfaces." (Marks, 2020) Turns out she had identified a new family of viruses. (Marks, 2020)

Almeida labeled this new family the coronavirus, from the Latin word "corona" meaning "crown," a nod to the spiky shape of the specimen. (Marks, 2020)

The mild symptoms associated with the coronavirus garnered little attention in the 1960s, but that didn't hold Almeida back from making a name for herself. She would go on to set the course for IEM techniques that enabled virologists to rapidly identify new viruses using clinical samples. (Marks, 2020)

Thanks to Almeida's contributions, to date seven coronaviruses have been identified as having the ability to transmit to humans.

During this time two coronaviruses were identified with symptomatology similar to the common cold. These viruses were considered "more of a nuisance than anything else" which initially landed them rather low on the list for research. (Williams, 2020)

All of this would change with the severe acute respiratory syndrome (SARS) outbreak which killed about 10 percent of the people it infected. (Broadbent, 2020) This virus was far deadlier than any coronavirus studied prior to 2003, infecting 774 individuals worldwide between 2002 and 2014. (Broadbent, 2020) While the exact source of the virus has never been proven, further studies discovered similar viruses were later found in bats.

Through a process known as cross-species transmission, or spillover, "viruses that infect one species can mutate in such a way that allows them to start infecting another species."

(Broadbent, 2020) Viruses transfer from species to species if they share the same host cell receptor—the protein on the surface of cells that enables viruses to bind and invade a host.

Viral spillover also caused the outbreaks of the Middle East Respiratory Syndrome (MERS) to occur in Saudi Arabia and South Korea. (Broadbent, 2020) While additional outbreaks of MERS pop up every year, they are usually well contained due to the low transmission rate. Additionally, "most of the cases have been linked to close contact with infected camels or very close contact with an already infected person." (Broadbent, 2020) In total there were 2,519 laboratory-confirmed cases of MERS and 866 deaths reported globally. (Broadbent, 2020)

Epidemiologists contain viruses like SARS and MERS much faster due to their low transmission rates. These experts are able to quantify how contagious a disease is through a measurement known as an R0 value. R0 values—pronounced "R naught"—indicate "the average number of people who will contract a contagious disease from one person with that disease." (Ramirez, 2020)

If an R0 value is less than one it means that the disease is on the decline, as each contagious person will cause less than one new infection. Conversely, if an R0 value is more than one "each existing infection causes more than one new infection." (Ramirez, 2020) In these cases the disease will continue to transmit between people and there is a potential for an epidemic.

For reference, the MERS transmission rate was less than one while the SARS R0 is estimated to be between two and three. (Broadbent, 2020) Recent estimates suggest that the transmission rate for SARS-CoV-2, the virus that causes COVID-19, is as high as five. (Broadbent, 2020)

Unlike COVID-19, SARS and MERS do not spread through presymptomatic transmission. This means individuals who have contracted these viruses are not contagious before their symptoms appear. (Broadbent, 2020) When symptoms do appear these patients often self-isolate or go to the hospital which limits transmission to the broader community.

"By and large, except for a couple of mass transmission events, almost all of the transmission of SARS was within the health care setting, when you have an aerosol-generating event like intubating someone or dialysis," explained Stephen Morse—an infectious disease epidemiologist at Columbia University's School of Public Health. (Rogers, 2020). SARS, therefore, could be controlled by managing infection control and prevention policies within hospitals. (Rogers, 2020)

Individuals infected with COVID-19 may feel well enough to take a flight, go to work, or even go to the gym, all the while unknowingly transmitting the virus to those around them.

National governments managed to contain SARS and MERS despite their high fatality rates (9.6 percent and 34 percent respectively) because their transmission rates were so low. (Rogers, 2020) The opposite would be true for swine flu—a virus with high transmission, but low fatality rates.

SWINE FLU (H1N1)

In 2009 a new version of the H1N1 influenza virus was detected. Commonly referred to as Swine Flu, the virus rapidly spread and is said to have killed anywhere from 151,700 to 575,400 people in the first twelve months, according to the Centers for Disease Control and Prevention. With an R0 between 1.4 and 1.6 the virus was highly infectious, however, unlike COVID-19, the fatality rate was very low. (Rogers, 2020)

"The 2009, H1N1 Swine Flu […] spread very, very well, but the fatality rate was quite low, and that's the reason why it wasn't dubbed as a particularly serious pandemic," Dr. Anthony Fauci explained. (Rogers, 2020) So while swine flu may have infected over one billion people by the end of 2010, the health outcomes associated with contracting the virus were not nearly as severe. (Rogers, 2020)

EBOLA

Like SARS and MERS, Ebola is quite severe when contracted but is fairly hard to contract. Unlike Swine Flu and COVID-19, Ebola is actually "hard to catch because it is spread through direct contact with the bodily fluid of an infected person, like blood, sweat, and urine." (Rogers, 2020) This form of transmission makes the virus much easier to trace, since only individuals in close contact with an infected person are at risk for contracting the virus.

Ebola symptoms are easily identifiable—including fever, fatigue, vomiting, and diarrhea—and individuals are only contagious once symptoms surface. (Rogers, 2020) This means individuals are aware when they are getting sick and can seek medical care before transmitting the disease to others.

"If you want to see illnesses which are controllable, they all have transmission very much tied to symptoms, and this includes SARS and Ebola," said William Hanage—an epidemiologist at the Harvard T.H. Chan School of Public Health. (Rogers, 2020)

The first Ebola virus surfaced in 1976, and since then there have been various outbreaks with the most recent in West Africa from 2014 to 2016. (Rogers, 2020) The World Health Organization estimates that the average case fatality rate is around 50 percent. Yet even with such high fatality only eleven thousand people died during 2014–2016, and the disease was largely contained to the same region where it was initially detected. (Rogers, 2020)

When symptoms and transmission are closely linked, track and trace procedures can be implemented to isolate individuals presenting symptoms and mitigate the spread of the disease.

For COVID-19 this could not be further from the case.

SARS-COV-2

On January 9, 2020, Chinese authorities reported a viral outbreak to the World Health Organization. The symptoms were diverse, and the virus was characterized by symptoms such as loss of taste or smell, sore throat, shortness of breath or difficulty breathing, fatigue, and cough. It was, of course, the novel coronavirus that would be known around the world as COVID-19.

Continued research would reveal that those infected with COVID-19 experience mild to moderate respiratory illness. The risk of serious illness is greater for individuals with underlying medical problems such as cardiovascular disease, diabetes, chronic respiratory disease, autoimmune disease, and cancer. (World Health Organization)

The virus spreads "primarily through droplets of saliva or discharge from the nose when an infected person coughs or sneezes." (World Health Organization) To prevent this transmission health authorities recommend adhering to social distancing guidelines and isolation for individuals who believe they have been exposed to the virus.

The virus has the worst traits an outbreak can have:

1. It is contracted through presymptomatic transmission.
2. The symptomology is covert, and symptoms may initially present as a different virus altogether—or perhaps never present at all.
3. "Individuals with underlying medical conditions are at increased risk for severe illness from the virus that causes COVID-19," the Centers for Disease Control and Prevention reports. This "severe illness" could mean hospitalization, admission to the ICU, intubation, mechanical ventilation, or death. Further, these underlying medical conditions range from diabetes and obesity to cancer and

certain heart conditions. (Centers for Disease Control and Prevention)

So on one hand, the disease is just mild enough that individuals can be presymptomatic, or asymptomatic, and unknowingly spread the virus to others without a trace. While on the other hand, the disease can result in symptoms so severe that it can lead to overloaded hospitals.

Take it from me, I had the virus and went around telling people they were "really bad allergies." Thankfully I followed my doctor's instructions and immediately quarantined once my symptoms advanced, but who knows how many individuals were infected by that time. Not only was I contagious when I thought the virus was my seasonal allergies, but I also could have been contagious days before I presented symptoms.

From an epidemiological standpoint this makes the disease extremely complex to track and contain, precisely because symptoms are not closely tied to transmission.

So how do you contain a disease like this? A disease that is the perfect storm of modern diseases. A disease that is just as contagious as H1N1, or swine flu, but not deadly enough to inspire adherence to public health directives?

Ibrahima Socé Fall—assistant director-general for emergencies response at the World Health Organization—describes a set of eight core elements of an outbreak response. (Fall, 2021)

First, you have to have a coordination mechanism in place, at the state and national levels, for rapid action. (Fall, 2021)

This means activating a central response hub to enable incident management and dynamic deployment of resources and interventions in response to viral transmission.

The second element of an outbreak response is health care intervention—the careful calibration of public health responses designed to address the specific impacts brought on by the outbreak. These interventions include case management activities, infection prevention and control activities, surveillance and disease intelligence activities, and community engagement.

Third is response team mobilization. Establishing an emergency response team is core to effectively combating an outbreak. Team members should bring multidisciplinary perspectives to develop a multifaceted response plan with clearly defined responsibilities, to drive accountability and enable rapid action.

Roles on this response team may include, but are not limited to: clinicians to support medical interventions, epidemiologists to analyze transmission patterns and assess the impacts of intervention responses, microbiologists to perform diagnostic testing on samples and define clinical protocols, infection prevention and control representatives to develop strategies for slowing the spread of the virus, social scientists to serve as the voice of patient populations, and logistics experts to optimize resource distribution and ensure adequate funds are available, "so supplies, transport, and human resources can be put in place in a rapid and effective manner." (Future Learn, 2019)

Fourth, you must mobilize your outbreak responses with the flexibility to adjust or pivot your plans based on real-time data or the latest science-backed insights on the transmission of the virus.

Alerting the international community—the fifth outbreak response—will be part of mobilizing your outbreak response to support knowledge and resource sharing, as different countries may be at different points of the curve. Learning from the international community only accelerates progress towards a contained virus. So, we all need to be in this together.

Sixth, as the virus matures so should your response. Dynamically adjusting activities and resources on the ground ensures strategies are adapted to address the needs of the local community.

Seventh, as these strategies are deployed specialists must monitor the effectiveness of their response by enabling real-time tracking of the virus and documenting the associated tactics that work best to contain it.

The eighth element of a response is outbreak documentation. Following the outbreak, "we need a broad evaluation [...] to document success stories, best practices, but also, lessons learned." (Fall, 2021)

This is how you hunt a virus. You pack your bag the night before with the tools you'll need to capture your target. You understand how your target moves and how it defends itself.

You study and observe to find weakness, and you exploit those weaknesses to prevail.

COVID-19 was a uniquely difficult target to contain and eliminate.

Our inadequate public health care infrastructure, national leadership, and emergency response were no match for a virus so uniquely destructive and challenging to contain. Our only course of action is to learn from our mistakes and become better hunters for the next time.

CHAPTER 3

WE SHOULD
LISTEN TO BILL

———

A decade after World War II the neighborhood of Wallingford, Washington, was a hotbed of new development. The
Seattle suburb had a thriving marine economy. The north
end of Lake Union bustled with hundreds of marine based
businesses, from fishing to water transportation, and by 1949
would be known as "one of the busiest and most highly developed industrial areas of the city." (Veith, 90)

The auto-oriented consumer population led to a rise in commercial business opportunities catering to newly mobile
shoppers. Parking lots were developed across the town. The
Northgate Mall, the first shopping experience of its kind,
opened in 1950 serving as a central hub for shopping and
entertainment. (Veith, 109)

During this time of prosperity, the Seattle Freeway project
received federal approval and funding in 1957. This initiative

would enable an improved transit system for consumers to commute to and from the employment centers downtown.

Amid the hustle and bustle of this developing city a covert project was brewing under the surface. Literally.

It was the height of the Cold War and as tensions rose between the United States and the Soviet Union the threat of a nuclear attack grew imminent. President Harry Truman issued the Federal Civil Defense Act of 1950, summoning local governments to prepare for an attack. (Becker, 2010) In schools children rehearsed duck-and-cover drills. In homes families stockpiled canned beans, preserved meats, and survival supplies. In Seattle, deep beneath Interstate 5, construction crews carved out a two-hundred-person fallout shelter. (Millman, 2019)

The nuclear fallout shelter beneath I-5 would be the only one of its kind anywhere in the world, and it would fill the land-scape of Bill Gates's childhood. The Gates family lived in a middle-class Wallingford home, just two miles from the construction site. It was there, in the shadow of an ever-present threat of mass destruction, that a young Gates watched his parents fill barrels with survival supplies and formed his world view.

The cofounder of Microsoft recalls that time in his life, when a nuclear war was the greatest threat facing the United States. In a 2015 TED talk, he warned his audience, "if anything kills over ten million people in the next few decades, it's most likely to be a highly infectious virus rather than a war. Not missiles, but microbes." (Gates, 2015)

While the United States has made heavy investments in nuclear deterrents, Gates argued, a similar investment has never been made to build up the infrastructure to combat a global pandemic.

During the Ebola crisis efforts to track the spread, report new cases, and identify treatment approaches were not well coordinated. (Gates, 2015) We did not have dedicated epidemiologists or a medical team ready to go. (Gates, 2015) The approach to stopping the spread was not digitally enabled; reports came in on paper, were very delayed in being posted online, and were mostly inaccurate. (Gates, 2015) We did not have a method for preparing impacted communities. (Gates, 2015)

We simply were not ready. We had no system in place. Because of these systemic shortcomings more than ten thousand people died.

The situation could have been much worse if it weren't for three factors. First, the work done by health care workers prevented the spread, thus minimizing infections and localizing the virus. (Gates, 2015) Second, the nature of the virus itself. Ebola is not an airborne virus. It is spread through the exchange of bodily fluids from an infected individual, and by the time an individual has contracted the virus, they are bedridden. (Gates, 2015) Lastly, the virus was largely contained in rural areas and did not reach densely populated urban centers. Believe it or not, we got lucky that time.

Next time, Gates forewarned, we might not be so lucky. Next time we might confront a virus capable of flying under the radar, a virus so stealthy "people feel well enough while they're infectious that they get on a plane or they go to a market." (Gates, 2015)

I was completely dumbfounded.

In 2015 Bill Gates knew we would not be prepared for the next outbreak.

Gates's cautionary tale echoed those of virology and infectious disease researchers around the world.

Over a decade before a novel coronavirus would cross continents and breach borders virologist Pardis Sabeti sounded an alarm. The global health community needed an early warning system, she said—one that could "detect and respond to emerging viral threats in real time." (Siliezar, 2020) Sabeti—a virologist at the Broad Institute of Harvard and MIT—has a track record of harvesting data to analyze infectious diseases and sharing her findings with the scientific community to inform public health interventions.

She won a Rhodes Scholarship in 1996 to study genetic resistance to infectious diseases at Oxford University. (Siliezar, 2020) By 2006 she developed an algorithm to enable scientists to examine the human genome for regions linked to infectious diseases. (Siliezar, 2020) In 2014, she was part of the team that diagnosed the first case of Ebola in West Africa and would later sequence the virus's genetic makeup. (Siliezar, 2020) Her work in the region would land her on *Time* magazine's "Person of the Year" issue.

Despite these accolades Sabeti struggled to convince sponsors to back her vision for Sentinel, a prospective early warning system for viral outbreaks.

If Sentinel received funding every American hospital would have received the genetic sequencing of SARS-CoV-2 on January 11, 2020—when Chinese scientists published the virus's genome. (Yong, 2020) This information would have allowed us to proactively create accurate tests, identify transmission patterns, and coordinate a public health response before the virus even arrived.

Dr. Kamran Khan had a similar vision after his experience as an epidemiologist treating patients in Toronto during the SARS outbreak in 2003. (Stieg, 2020)

The ordeal lasted for six months, killed a total of 774 people across twenty-nine countries, and cost approximately $40 billion globally, as estimated by the Centers for Disease Control. (Stieg, 2020) Reflecting on his takeaways from the SARS epidemic Khan said, "Let's not get caught flatfooted, let's anticipate rather than react." (Stieg, 2020) He goes on, in his CNBC interview, to describe how the medical community cannot always rely on government agencies to report information as timely as is required.

Khan began exploring alternative methods to collect information on infectious disease activity.

For the next decade he studied how infectious diseases spread globally and founded BlueDot. (Stieg, 2020) Named after scientist Carl Sagan's description of Earth from NASA's

Voyager 1 in 1990, BlueDot is "a proprietary software-as-a--service designed to track, locate, and conceptualize infectious disease spread." (Stieg, 2020) BlueDot uses artificial intelligence to interpret data from hundreds of thousands of data sources—such as statements from official public health organizations, digital media, global airline ticketing data, livestock health reports, and population demographics—and sends out alerts to health care, government, business, and public health clients when disease outbreaks are detected. (Stieg, 2020)

This data-driven approach enables the company to rapidly ingest and process troves of data every fifteen minutes—twenty-four hours a day and seven days a week.

As the data comes in a team of physicians and computer programmers on standby translate the findings into a consolidated report, distributed to clients across health care, public health, government, and business sectors. Khan explains, "We don't use artificial intelligence to replace human intelligence, we basically use it to find the needles in the haystack and present them to our team." (Stieg, 2020)

BlueDot not only detects infectious disease threats earlier than other sources but also assesses the impacts of pathogen transmission and forecasts how the disease may spread globally.

The team achieved these goals by detecting the COVID-19 virus.

On December 30, 2019, the platform "picked up on a cluster of 'unusual pneumonia' cases happening around a market in Wuhan, China, and flagged it." (Stieg, 2020) Nine days before WHO would release a statement BlueDot had correctly identified what would come to be known as COVID-19.

Using global airline ticketing and other available data, BlueDot's algorithms correctly predicted cities with the highest volume of travelers coming from Wuhan including Bangkok, Hong Kong, Tokyo, Taipei, Phuket, Seoul, and Singapore. (Stieg, 2020) Ultimately, these cities would be the first to be hit by the virus.

Government agencies would have been more equipped to respond to the demands of this pandemic if they had access to these predictive capabilities.

Taking stock of how our emergency preparedness faltered in this pandemic can serve as a powerful blueprint for the next crisis. Tools like the Global Response Index can help us calibrate future response strategies using a quantitative approach.

Foreign Policy Analytics (FPA) developed the Global Response Index to monitor, assess, and rank global responses to the pandemic. The tool calculates a consolidated score for a country's response by measuring activity across three categories: COVID-19 public health directives, financial responses, and fact-based communications and accountability by political leaders. (Foreign Policy, 2021)

The FPA team monitors eight public health categories to assess a country's health response. These include stay-at--home directives, public gathering restrictions, cancellation of public events, testing policies, COVID-19 tests per thousand people, emergency health care expenditures, travel restrictions, and contact-tracing capabilities. (Foreign Policy, 2021)

Countries with the highest scores across these categories have mitigated the spread of the virus by limiting population movement, making tests widely accessible, funding the distribution of PPE (personal protective equipment) and COVID-19 related medical supplies, and tracking exposures to implement strict isolation protocols.

Public health directives alone do not drive a strong response to COVID-19. Economies around the world have been disrupted by the safety measures required to slow the spread of the pandemic. An April issue of *Time* magazine suggests the total cost of the pandemic might be as high as $4.1 trillion— roughly 5 percent of global gross domestic product—due to the global disruption of consumption, investment, and tourism. (Alegado, 2020)

To account for a country's ability to address the economic impacts of the pandemic the Global Response Index evaluates government subsidies such as stimulus packages, income support, and forbearance policies. These financial interventions indicate a nation's commitment to stimulating the economy and relieving individuals and businesses of the economic burden of the pandemic. (Alegado, 2020)

The third and final component factored into a country's government response score examines a country's ability to communicate fact-based information and promote freedom of the press on matters pertaining to COVID-19. As stated on their website, the Global Response Index is the only assessment tool for government responses to COVID-19 that includes this metric and according to the team "was considered critical for inclusion, given the impact that national leadership's public communication has on individuals' and groups' actions that ultimately contribute to or mitigate the virus' spread." (Foreign Policy, 2021)

As discussed in the previous chapter, social mobilization and community engagement must be planned for all health directives to ensure people not only adhere to the safety measures implemented at local, state, and federal levels but also understand why these interventions are being prescribed.

To quantify fact-based communications the tool measures eight topics associated with disinformation related to the coronavirus. These range from the conspiracy purporting coronavirus is caused by 5G to claims that the coronavirus is a man-made weapon.

An Oxford University study found that a disconcertingly high portion of adults in England did not agree with science or government-backed facts on the coronavirus. The study uncovered that 60 percent of adults in England believe to some extent that the government is misleading the public about the cause of the virus and 40 percent believe that to some extent the spread of the virus is a deliberate attempt by powerful people to gain control. (Oxford University, 2020) This lack of institutional trust poses a real threat to public health, as the individuals who believe in these conspiracies may be less likely to comply with government directives aimed at slowing the spread of the virus.

By incorporating these metrics into their scoring framework, the FPA team assesses how disinformation on the virus may contribute to a country's inability to effectively slow the spread.

The fact-based communication and accountability section also measures freedom of the press. Leveraging data from the International Press Institute (IPI), the index determines whether a country has engaged in any of the following four media limitations based on COVID-19 reporting: arrests or charges of journalists, restrictions on access to information, censorship, and fake news regulations. (Foreign Policy, 2021) Freedom of the press is acknowledged as a critical tool for dispersing fact-based communication to the general population and is considered a vital component of an emergency response.

Combined, public health directives, economic relief packages, and fact-based communication are the key ingredients for a holistic response to the COVID-19 pandemic. The data provided in the Global Response Index provides a standard framework to analyze the strategies effective at tackling COVID-19. In the future this data has the potential to play a proactive role in assessing performance across these categories in real time.

What would our world look like now if Sabeti received funding for Sentinel years ago? If Khan's early detection of the virus was used to coordinate a global health response? If we had a dynamic dashboard that tracked and monitored the metrics available in the Global Response Index?

Bill Gates was right—we weren't ready. We should have been. We probably even could have been. Next time we must be.

Our lives depend on it.

CHAPTER 4

THE PANDEMIC SURVIVAL GUIDE

———

Back in middle school, my friends and I used to play a board game called *Pandemic*.

We pretended to be disease-fighting experts tasked with saving the world from several infectious diseases. As a team we set up research stations, treated patients, and discovered cures for diseases. We were unified in our mission: cure the viruses faster than they could spread.

If this game were to be played as a COVID-19 outbreak simulator, each player would represent a different country and each country would start at a different point in the game.

***

New Zealand, Saudi Arabia, and Iceland responded proactively to the first signs of crisis.

NEW ZEALAND

Prime minister Jacinda Ardern had a monumental task ahead of her. The New Zealand Prime Minister wondered how she might avoid the fate predicted by the models in front of her and how she could avoid more than a thousand new cases of COVID-19 a day. (Taylor, 2020) When the virus breached the country's border in February 2020 Ardern sprang into action. By March the country entered a level three lockdown. (Taylor, 2020)

"Non-essential businesses were closed, discretionary domestic air travel was banned, and all events and gatherings had to be cancelled." (Taylor, 2020) Yet that was not enough.

Forty-eight hours later the country entered a level four lockdown. This was crunch time. The eliminate policy mandated citizens only maintain contact with individuals in their home. (Taylor, 2020)

The country quickly scaled testing capacity and as early as May could process up to eight thousand tests per day, giving New Zealand one of the highest testing rates per capita in the world. (Taylor, 2020)

By October 2020 New Zealand had largely eradicated the virus. (Taylor, 2020) As of January 11, 2021, New Zealand had registered a total of 2,222 COVID-19 cases and twenty-five fatalities resulting from the virus. This still was not enough.

Ardern thought beyond the current crisis and set up a fund—totaling approximately 17 percent of GDP—designed to reduce the unemployment rate over the next two years.

(Bremmer, 2021) The revised budgeting approach will shift the government from a surplus to a deficit over the next two years, but this is an investment Ardern is willing to make to ensure a comprehensive recovery for her country. (Bremmer, 2021)

SAUDI ARABIA

Saudi Arabia set the foundation for their COVID-19 response years before their first case.

The Vision 2030 National Transformation Program accelerated massive investments in digital infrastructure across the country's health care, education, and other social service systems predating the virus. (Hassounah et al, 2020)

With the largest social media user population in the world per capita, the nation harnessed these virtual channels to push online campaigns and provision health care services, education, telecommunication, commerce, and risk communication. (Hassounah et al, 2020) This innovative approach to cascading fact-based communication to the public led the country to develop and launch nineteen apps and platforms to support the distribution of essential resources amidst strict lockdown and viral containment regulations.

The pandemic "tested the reliability of the country's digital infrastructure and has highlighted questionable gaps for decision makers. This has been a nationwide trial of Saudi citizens' acceptance and ability to use and engage with the digitalization of these services and communications," experts explained. (Hassounah et al, 2020)

ICELAND

Like Saudi Arabia and New Zealand, Iceland also benefited from an early response to the outbreak augmented by a tailored package of government resources to promote containment of, and education on, the deadly virus.

It all started somewhere along Kári Stefánsson's morning commute. As founder of a company specializing in the human genome, Stefánsson devours data. So, on that morning in March 2020, his attention was piqued by a radio report on the latest COVID-19 data. The World Health Organization, the announcer said, estimated that 3.4 percent of people infected with SARS-CoV-2 would die. (Scudellari, 2020)

"I couldn't figure out how they could calculate [that number] out without knowing the spread of the virus," Stefánsson recalls. (Scudellari, 2020)

The founder of deCODE, an Iceland-based company specializing in the human genome, Stefánsson believed effectively tracking the spread of the virus required monitoring all cases—even when infections were mild or asymptomatic.

From his perspective, to effectively contain the virus it was critical to track how the contagion spread in populations and document clear, data-driven observations on transmission patterns. With this information countries would be better equipped to develop dynamic response plans that could be configured and optimized as the virus evolved.

When he reached his office Stefánsson called Iceland's Directorate of Health and offered deCODE's resources to track the spread of the virus. Stefánsson's proposal was met with a "For Heaven's sake do that" from government officials. (Scudellari, 2020)

deCODE and the government entered into a joint partnership for the next nine months. "The teams have tracked the health of every person who has tested positive for SARS--CoV-2, sequenced the genetic material of each viral isolate, and screened more than half of the island's 368,000 residents for infection." (Scudellari, 2020)

Iceland centered their response on big data. Constantly analyzing large swaths of information positioned the country to publish early findings on how the pathogen spread through populations. (Scudellari, 2020)

Iceland discovered "almost half of infected people are asymptomatic, that children are much less likely to become sick than adults and that the most common symptoms of mild COVID-19 are muscle aches, headaches and a cough—not fever." (Scudellari, 2020)

The intimate collaboration between public and private sectors enabled the Icelandic government to rapidly develop testing competencies such that hospitals were testing individuals arriving from abroad a month before the first case was identified. (Partridge-Hicks, 2020)

deCODE programmers supported the development and launch of software empowering citizens, even those with the mildest symptoms, to sign up to be tested. At the testing center residents show a barcode from their phone which is then used to automatically print a unique label for a swab sample. (Scudellari, 2020) Then, the magic happens.

The sample is sent to a lab at deCODE's headquarters and processed jointly by the university hospital and deCODE. Individuals receive confirmation via text if they are negative, and if they are positive, they are automatically "enrolled in a tele-health monitoring service at a COVID outpatient clinic for a fourteen-day isolation period." (Scudellari, 2020) At this clinic patients receive ongoing calls from nurses or physicians who carefully document their medical history and symptoms and log that information into a national electronic medical record system.

Documenting this information in a structured way allowed the country to leverage this data to inform ongoing research efforts.

At the same time, labs would test each sample "for the amount of virus it contains, which has been used as an indicator for contagiousness and severity of illness." (Scudellari, 2020) The samples are also comprehensively analyzed to determine the strain of the virus and track its origin.

By November 2020 Iceland tested 55 percent of the country's total population and was able to distill insights from ongoing research to dynamically adjust medical interventions in the country. For example, "individuals showing any sign of a common cold or aches [were] encouraged to get tested, and the hospital categorized new patients into one of three stages according to their symptoms [to dictate] their level of care." (Scudellari, 2020)

This visionary approach to containing the virus prevented the country from having to implement a full lockdown, saving lives and the country's tourist-based economy.

Iceland had an enviable advantage in the war against COVID-19 with science at the nucleus of their pandemic response. This strategy provided the country with a blueprint for future pandemic responses.

For countries like Senegal, South Korea, and Taiwan, lessons learned from previous outbreaks would guide the path forward.

SENEGAL

With a fragile health care system characterized by a high infant mortality rate, scarcity of hospital beds, and roughly seven doctors for every one hundred thousand people, Senegal has proven that it does not take a wealth of resources to respond aggressively to the COVID-19 virus. (Shesgreen, 2020)

With a population of sixteen million the country had reported only 14,982 cases and 311 total deaths as of October 1, 2020. The director of Senegal's Health Emergency Operation Center, Dr. Abdoulaye Bousso, said the country began developing contingency plans as soon as WHO declared the coronavirus an international public health emergency in January 2020. (Partridge-Hicks, 2020)

When the first positive COVID-19 case was detected on March 2, 2020, the Senegalese government responded swiftly and strongly by implementing a curfew, restricting all domestic travel, and imposing a strict stay-at-home order. The country also benefited from quickly expanding testing capacity by developing mobile labs, many of which could provide test results within twenty-four hours, with some boasting turnaround times as fast as two hours. (Shesgreen, 2020) Hotels were transformed into quarantine units, and in Dakar, Senegal, there have been prototypes developed for a ventilator that could cost as low as $160 to address the mass global shortage of these devices. (Petesch, 2020)

For those who watched how the Senegalese government handled an Ebola outbreak in 2014, this response comes as no surprise.

The WHO publicly announced West Africa's Ebola epidemic on March 23, 2014.

Originating in Meliandou, Guinea—a small, remote village—the virus rapidly evolved with forty-nine cases and twenty-nine deaths reported by the time the WHO formally announced the outbreak on their website. (World Health Organization, 2021) The first case did not arrive in Senegal until August 29, 2014, however, with the "outbreaks raging just across its borders, Senegal was well-prepared, with a detailed response plan in place." (World Health Organization, 2021)

When the deadly virus would reach the Senegalese border, it would arrive in Dakar—home to the world-class Pasteur Institute of Dakar, a fully approved WHO laboratory equipped to test biosafety level IV pathogens like Ebola. (World Health Organization, 2021) With these resources so close at hand the WHO dispatched three senior epidemiologists who worked collaboratively with public health officials in Senegal to track and contain the virus. (World Health Organization, 2021)

With only a single case detected the country immediately mobilized a rapid nationwide response led by a locally funded National Crisis Committee which served as the hub for emergency response for the country. Additionally, the country set up a humanitarian corridor in Dakar to facilitate the provision of critical resources such as food, medicines, and other essential supplies into the country from humanitarian agencies. (World Health Organization, 2021)

Eight days after the first case was confirmed the individual who brought the virus from Guinea to Dakar tested negative for this strain of the Ebola virus. Despite this recovery, rigorous contact-tracing measures continued to ensure the spread had been stymied. With a total of seventy-four close contacts identified, the government continually monitored their symptoms twice daily and instituted testing procedures. With all results negative the government continued instituting safety protocols, and after forty-two days the country had effectively eradicated the disease. (World Health Organization, 2021)

As summarized in a WHO article highlighting the Senegalese government's success in handling the epidemic, Dr. Coll-Seck—then health minister—attributes the country's success in containing the virus to the following actions:

- Strong political leadership at the highest level.
- Early detection and response facilitated by a detailed plan and quickly activated National Crisis Committee.
- Increased surveillance at the country's main points of entry.
- Rapid mobilization of domestic and international resources.
- Operational partnerships such as the WHO.
- Fact-based nationwide public awareness campaigns.
- Coordinated collaboration across all government ministries supported by ongoing community engagement.
- Direct support to patient contacts, in the form of money, food, and psychological counseling, as a critical incentive for cooperation and compliance; followed by continued support of these patients as they reintegrated into society.

These measures provided the country with an invaluable road map that would guide their approach to addressing the coronavirus pandemic just six years later.

I found similar patterns in South Korea and Taiwan.

SOUTH KOREA

Leveraging key insights gained from the 2015 MERS epidemic the South Korean government activated the economic and technological resources at their disposal to keep domestic fatality low, while also playing a critical role in international efforts to slow the spread of the virus. With a total population of approximately fifty-two million people South Korea reported 23,812 COVID-19 cases and 413 deaths as of October 1, 2020; that is .046 percent of the country's total population compared to the 7 percent of Americans who have contracted the virus. While the country's caseload was relatively low, "South Korea began developing COVID-19 tests and scaling up production to thousands-per-day," exporting surplus tests and supplies internationally. (Bremmer, 2021)

Rather than shut the economy down the government opted to deploy real-time tracking technologies for COVID-19 patients paired with social distancing guidelines, and an extensive testing and contact-tracing infrastructure. Citizens also received a substantial government stimulus, with $12.2 billion provided to businesses and citizens in the early spring, and an additional $6.5 billion provided in September to go along with $230 billion of support in the form of loans and guarantees. (Soendergaard Larsen, 2020)

It is estimated that the financial stimulus as a share of the country's Gross Domestic Product—the monetary value of finished goods and services bought by an end-user—is a whopping 5.4 percent. Experts believe that because this progressive fiscal response was deployed early on in the outbreak, it boosted consumption and improved market conditions as "more businesses were open to spend those cash payouts […] which translated to South Korean consumers spending more and saving less of their bailout checks." (Soendergaard Larsen, 2020) The stimulus actually stimulated the South Korean economy resulting in a year-over-year increase in consumption and record approval ratings for president Moon Jae-in. (Soendergaard Larsen, 2020; Bremmer, 2021)

With advanced knowledge of the dynamics at play in a pandemic, the South Korean government was able to quickly respond to the fiscal and public health demands of COVID-19, while also playing a critical role as an international partner in sharing resources.

TAIWAN

Similar to South Korea, Taiwan's response to COVID-19 was guided by the epidemic response plan the country developed in response to the 2003 SARS outbreak.

Rather than shutting down the economy the Taiwanese government "used contact tracing and mobile Sim-tracking to identify and ensure those in quarantine were actually abiding by the rules." (Bremmer, 2021) Medical officials also held daily briefings for the public and businesses were required to use strict precautionary measures—such as taking temperatures and offering hand sanitizer—before patrons were allowed to enter. (Bremmer, 2021) This centralized response was supported by a single-payer health care system and a vice president who moonlights as an epidemiologist. The results speak for themselves. With a total population of around twenty-four million the country reported only 514 cases and seven deaths as of October 1, 2020.

The Taiwan and South Korea case studies highlight another trend among countries with a strong outbreak response: the more centralized the health care infrastructure in a country, it seems, the better coordinated their response.

THE ADVANTAGES OF CENTRALIZED HEALTH CARE

Back in April the Council on Foreign Relations—a United States nonprofit think tank specializing in foreign policy and international affairs—published an analysis on the efficacy of six health care systems at addressing the COVID-19 pandemic. The report found that the Taiwanese single-payer system—characterized by a single government insurance plan with comprehensive benefits for primary care, hospital services, prescription drugs, and other critical medical interventions—effectively responded to contain the virus. The government's ability to provide free coronavirus tests and require that hospitals test patients at the earliest sign of symptoms enabled early management of the pathogen. (Maizland et al, 2020)

While South Korea has a public-private system—meaning that citizens are covered by the government sponsored National Health Insurance program while health care services are delivered through the private sector—the report still found that their response was swift compared to peers.

The South Korean government was able to rapidly develop and deploy a diagnostic test upon detection of the first case in January 2020. (Maizland et al 2020) In addition, the government was able to take advantage of their close relationship with hospitals and "designated specific hospitals for COVID-19 patients [...] [requiring] patients seeking other medical care to visit non-COVID-19 hospitals." (Maizland et al, 2020) The government was also able to effectively organize the private sector to produce medical supplies for public consumption. The centralized health care structure enabled the South Korean government to quickly mobilize the medical infrastructure required to organize a swift response to the outbreak.

Similarly, Australia's universal public health insurance program is funded by the federal government. However, their hybrid system also allows, and encourages, citizens to purchase insurance from private insurers who offer coverage for hospital and ambulance services as well as general care. (Maizland et al, 2020) With a total of 27,063 cases of COVID-19 and 882 related deaths as of October 1, 2020, Australia has prevailed as a country frequently ranked highly for their epidemic preparedness and response. (Foreign Policy, 2021) Even with strict social containment policies the prime minister, Scott Morrison, recognized that if the virus got out of hand "intensive care units could become overwhelmed [in a matter of] weeks." (Foreign Policy, 2021) In anticipation, the government moved thousands of hospital beds, doctors, and nurses out of private hospitals and into the public system. In addition, the country had one of the highest testing rates per capita, which protected the country from untraced transmission.

These three examples highlight the power of a coordinated health care system amidst a global pandemic. Although each country had a slightly different health care model, a country's centralized approach enabled the government to respond to the increasing demands of a global pandemic quickly and dynamically.

***

The *Pandemic* board game of my youth was not a zero-sum game: we all won, or we all lost. Fighting a pandemic in the real world requires global cooperation and a unified mission too. This isn't *Monopoly*—you can't cash in at the end. If even one player—one country—tries to make a play for a profit, the consequences may be catastrophic across the board. No one wins unless we all win. The virus will not have been contained until we've all contained it.

While this virus may be on the decline the next virus could be around the corner. To prepare we must work cooperatively to make strategic decisions, allocate resources, and respond to the latest, soundest scientific information as the virus advances.

It's up to us to determine how the game will end.

PART II

THE RECKONING

CHAPTER 5

REMEMBER
THEIR NAMES

———

Breonna Taylor. George Floyd. Elijah McClain. Theirs are three of the Black lives for whom protestors took to the streets to demand justice in 2020—Black lives that matter. Say their names.

When seventeen-year-old Trayvon Martin died with a hoodie on his back and a bag of Skittles in his hand President Barack Obama said his name. When a Florida jury acquitted the man who shot and killed the unarmed teen President Obama said his name again. "Trayvon Martin could have been me thirty-five years ago." (Memmott, 2013)

"There are very few African-American men in this country who haven't had the experience of being followed when they go shopping," the forty-fourth president of the United States told a national television audience. "That includes me." (Memmott, 2013)

Many Black men have heard car locks click when they cross a street, the president said, "That's happened to me." Experiences like these, he explained, "inform how the African-American community interprets what happened one night in Florida." (Memmott, 2013)

Being Black in America can feel like you're assumed guilty before proven innocent. This reality is traumatic and often tragic. Out of the Trayvon Martin tragedy emerged a movement. The Black Lives Matter Global Network Foundation vowed to "build local power to intervene in violence inflicted on Black communities by the state vigilantes" as the man who killed the seventeen-year-old child walked away unscathed. (Black Lives Matter, 2021)

An observational study on police arrests between 1997 to 2008 indicates that "nearly 50 percent of Black males, and 44 percent of Latinx males, are arrested by the age of twenty-three." (Schindler et al, 2020)

In 2017 alone, Black individuals between the ages of twenty and twenty-four were killed by law enforcement at more than triple the rate of their white counterparts. (Schindler et al, 2020) In 2018 Black men in their mid-twenties were twenty times more likely to be incarcerated than white males. (Schindler et al, 2020) Overall, Black men are 2.5 times more likely to be killed by police than white men and in 2019 police killings ranked as the sixth leading cause of death for Black men and boys. (Aviles, 2020)

Similar patterns persist among Black women as well. While they represent "13 percent of the women population in the

United States, they represent 20 percent of women killed by police and nearly 30 percent who are killed while unarmed." (Brown et al, 2020) Most disturbing is about 36 percent of women killed by police died in their homes. (Brown et al, 2020)

These are the statistics the Black Lives Matter Global Network Foundation is up against. These are the odds Black people face every day.

In 2020 Black Lives Matter became a global rallying cry against systemic oppression and institutional racism for marginalized populations around the world. These statistics were no longer occasional features on the news as they had become real people whose deaths we had witnessed on our phones.

As we sat in our homes, quarantined from a virus that attacked the respiratory system, we heard George Floyd gasp, "I can't breathe." For eight minutes and fifteen seconds we watched a white police officer use his knee to choke the life out of another Black man.

Those eight minutes and fifteen seconds changed us.

The shared experience of bearing witness to those eight minutes and fifteen seconds gave way to a radical empathy that made the Black Lives Matter Movement palpable for the average American.

Despite seven years of grassroots organizing and activism, the Black Lives Matter protests of 2020 felt different. Amidst a global health crisis and economic downturn an estimated fifteen million to twenty-six million people in the United States alone participated in demonstrations demanding justice for Black lives lost due to police brutality—making these protests the largest movement in United States' history.

I am a Black woman who minored in African-American studies in college, and even I was shocked by these statistics. I wanted to understand why all of this was happening now. Why people from all walks of life suddenly felt so connected to these tragedies. Why my Instagram feed was suddenly flooded with messages like "Say Her Name" and "Defund the Police". Frankly, I wanted to know why people cared.

Nothing new was happening. Marginalized communities have been systemically monitored, targeted, and murdered by agents of white supremacy for centuries. Why was everyone paying attention now?

These movements gained traction not despite but rather because of the pandemic. Political scientists at Wellesley College think they know why. In a recent study they observed that "respondents who reported that they had been hurt financially by the pandemic were also substantially more likely to report that they had attended a protest and posted positively about the protests or BLM." (Arora, 2020)

This behavioral research suggests that ruptures in the American economy and disillusionment with the federal government expanded public interest in subversion of the status quo. This created a broader, more diverse base of recruits interested in championing a counterculture agenda.

The pandemic exposed previously protected, or privileged, groups to the harsh realities of systemic injustice. Four health equity experts leverage Critical Race Theory (CRT) to unpack how the COVID-19 pandemic has accelerated a more liberal political agenda. (Lang, 2020)

Critical Race Theory is a movement that began in 1989 dedicated to studying and transforming the relationship among race, racism, and power. The framework is composed of three tenets: intersectionality, centering the margins, and the social construction of race. (Morse et al, 2020)

Intersectionality is the concept that "individual or group experiences of oppression cannot be distilled into a single identity, such as either female or Black for Black women." (Morse et al, 2020) Centering the margins describes an intentional focus on marginalized perspectives. The social construction of race acknowledges racial classifications are socially defined and not biologically determined.

CRT is a framework that contextualizes and contends with the systemic racism that built this country. The theory "posits that racism remains pervasive and ordinary in the United States, impacts all aspects of society, and is seamlessly embedded in policies and social life." (Morse et al, 2020)

How is racism systematically embedded in our policies and social life? How is racism maintained and who benefits from it? We must be explicit answering these questions.

Racism existed before the concept of race was ever defined. Yes, you read that correctly. In fact, not only did racism exist before race but also was used to justify the very existence of race.

When colonists came to North America to establish a new society, they needed a workforce to support their developing economy. Prior to the mid-1600s the labor market represented a blend of European indentured servants and enslaved indigenous people who "worked side-by-side and co-mingled socially." (Roediger, 2021)

However, in the 1600s as the colonies matured it became less economically profitable to depend on indentured servants as the primary source of labor. State legislatures enacted strict laws to codify chattel slavery on the basis of race. Virginia's 1622 partus sequitur ventrem (often translated as "that which is born follows the womb") was enacted which "deviated from English common law, which assigned the legal status of children based on their father's legal status. Thus, children of enslaved women would automatically share the legal status of 'slave.'" (Roediger, 2021) Not only did this doctrine increase the enslaved population but also sanctioned the exploitation of enslaved women by the white planter population. (Roediger, 2021)

"The effects of the institution of slavery on American commerce were monumental—3.2 million slaves were worth $1.3 billion in market value, almost equal to the entire gross national product," professor Mehrsa Baradaran explains in her book, *The Color of Money: Black Banks and the Racial Wealth Gap.* (Baradaran, 10) The exploitation of Black labor yielded immense profit for the country, creating a toxic cycle whereby "growing international demand for cotton fueled the growth of slavery, and the legal and political arms of the state maintained and protected it." (Baradaran, 10)

The federal government institutionalized anti-Blackness to justify the institution of slavery and established a racial hierarchy to prevent coalitions from forming between the enslaved population and the white working class.

Bacon's Rebellion of 1676 highlights how the threat of solidarity between a Black and white working class could endanger the system of slavery and, therefore, the underpinnings of American commerce. With hopes of acquiring land previously reserved for Virginia's indigenous community "coalitions of poor white people, free and enslaved Africans, rebelled against the rising planter class." (Roediger, 2021) The threat of intersectional coalitions led elite white colonists to enact laws and social codes to police racial interactions and create a hierarchical system on the basis of "appearance, place of origin, and heredity." (Roediger, 2021)

This racial discourse was heightened during the Enlightenment, a period whereby European politics, philosophy, science, and communications were radically reoriented as "the false notion that 'white' people were inherently smarter, more capable, and more human than nonwhite people became accepted worldwide." (Roediger, 2021) Over centuries this belief system would justify colonization and lay the philosophical groundwork for chattel slavery. (Roediger, 2021)

These essentialist arguments—the notion that every individual has a set of attributes that are necessary to their identity and ability—would be put to the test during, and following, the War of Independence. "After the Revolution, the U.S. Constitution strongly encoded the protection of property within its words [...] the paradox of liberty—the human right to freedom and the socially protected rights to property—became the foundation and essence of the American consciousness." (Roediger, 2021) The hypocrisy of newly developed colonies seeking freedom from British rule as they continued to justify the institution of slavery created new legal avenues through which African Americans might pursue emancipation.

The transatlantic slave trade was disbanded in 1808, but the American system of slavery remained intact—fueled by pseudoscientific propaganda. (Roediger, 2021) For example, "Dr. Samuel Morton is infamous for his measurements of skulls across populations. He concluded that African people had smaller skulls and were therefore not as intelligent as others [...] [this notion was] built on by scientists such as Josiah Nott and Louis Agassiz [...] [both who] concluded that Africans were a separate species." (Roediger, 2021)

The disconnect between the concepts of freedom represented in the Constitution and the legally sanctioned subjugation of Black people required the federal government to step in and provide further clarity on the rights enslaved individuals could claim. (Roediger, 2021)

It is in this political environment that the landmark Dred Scott v. Sandford takes place. Dred Scott and his wife argued that they should be emancipated on the basis that they were moved, by their owners, to a free state. Ultimately, however, the Supreme Court would rule that the suit could not be brought to Federal Court on the basis that the claimants were not citizens according to the United States Constitution. This decision would send three damaging signals to perspective litigants and interested stakeholders: Black people were not citizens, they possessed no constitutional rights, and were considered property as outlined in the Constitution.

This is also the political and legal atmosphere in which the Underground Railroad gains traction, as a network of secret safe houses was established to guide enslaved individuals North in search of asylum and emancipation. The success of the Underground Railroad contributed to the growing regional divide between the North and the South— driven by combating views on the future of slavery in the country. Central to these divergent viewpoints was "the economies of slavery and political control of that system." (PBS, 2020)

The election of Abraham Lincoln would ultimately seal the fate of the Southern economy, leading to secession and the bloodiest conflict in the history of North America. (PBS, 2020) But "even though the Civil War decimated the South, the ill-gotten spoils of slavery remained and grew in the former cotton empires in America and Europe for generations." (Baradaran, 15) And while the Emancipation Proclamation would end the institution of slavery in the rebel states, the vestiges of slavery were perpetuated through a loophole in this executive order: that slavery could be used as a punishment for crime.

Historian Khalil Muhammad explains the impact of this exception, explaining how "all expressions of Black freedom, political rights, economic rights, and social rights were then subject to criminal sanction. Whites could accuse Black people who wanted to vote of being criminals. People who wanted to negotiate fair labor contracts could be defined as criminals. And the only thing that wasn't criminalized was the submission to a white landowner to work on their land." (North, 2020)

The criminal justice system became a mechanism through which white supremacists could, once again, exploit Black labor for profit. External contractors privatized this labor, to continue driving low costs, which continued to promote an economic model predicated on the subjugation of Black communities for profit. In parallel, census data told a very different story.

In prisons across the South, Black inmates outnumbered their white counterparts three to one in 1890 according to the United States Census Bureau. (North, 2020) Without the appropriate context the results of these objective social studies indicated that the newly emancipated population was *prone* to criminal behavior. There was never an investigation into the alleged crimes this population committed or the legal system that prosecuted these crimes, and so these facts were taken at face value and dangerous conclusions were drawn about how Black communities were acclimating to life post-slavery. (North, 2020)

Echoing essentialist sentiments from the Enlightenment, white supremacists argued that there was a crime problem endemic to the Black community that warranted reduced citizenship rights. Against this backdrop the criminalization of Black people "becomes the most dominant basis for justifying segregation [...] [defining] the heart of the Jim Crow form of segregation [...] [and shaping] the maldistribution of public goods for Black people .[...] And, of course, all of these restrictions are enforced by white citizens but most especially by local law enforcement, by police officers." (North, 2020)

Simply put, the police were tasked with enforcing strict social codes designed to regulate the interactions between white and Black populations. In doing so, the police become a critical tool for mitigating Black mobility by ensuring access to public goods and the accumulation of wealth was an exclusive right of white hegemony.

While it is difficult to pinpoint the exact origins of centralized municipal police departments, "urban evidence, [suggests] that such policing evolved from older systems of militias, sheriffs, constables, and night watches" who were responsible for upholding the institution of slavery by capturing "runaways" and responding to "unrest." (Hubert et al, 2020) As these police departments became more formalized in the late nineteenth century, specifically in highly populated urban centers, "officers were expected to control a 'dangerous underclass' that included African Americans, immigrants and the poor." (Hassett-Walker, 2020)

By controlling marginalized communities, white supremacists continued to profit in the cotton industry and thus "the criminal and legal system of the South was used to prevent the free movement of Blacks in the market." (Baradaran, 18)

Formal segregation provided another method for bypassing emancipation legislation. As legitimized by the 1896 Plessy v. Ferguson case, "separate but equal" was upheld as constitutional on the basis that segregation did not violate the equal protection clause of the Fourteenth Amendment. But if two public goods are equal, why did they need to be separate?

Moreover, *how* could these public goods be equal when white institutions had centuries to accumulate the resources to cultivate these public goods?

These are the questions that would fuel the Civil Rights Movement.

Control also manifested in violence. Lynchings, or extrajudicial murders by mob, were used as an intimidation tactic by white supremacists (primarily used in the South) to control Black communities.

This racial violence paired with the lack of accountability against lynching mobs would become the basis for the founding of the NAACP, the National Association for the Advancement of Colored People, in 1910. Outrage against lynchings would lead to a series of race riots whereby Black community members demanded justice for these unlawful murders, and white community members perpetuated the intimidation and violence of lynchings by retaliating and terrorizing Black communities for demanding justice.

Sound familiar? Just wait.

Cities decimated by these riots would commission studies to investigate the root cause of this unrest. Khalil Muhammad summarizes the results of a Chicago commission:

> *In that report, the Chicago commission [concludes] that there was systemic participation in mob violence by the police, and that when police officers had the choice to protect Black people from white mob violence, they chose to either aid and abet white mobs or to disarm Black people or to arrest them. And a number of people testify, all of whom are white criminal justice officials, that the police are systematically engaging in racial bias when they're targeting Black suspects, and more likely to arrest them and to book them on charges that they wouldn't do for a white man. (North, 2020)*

That's right. This report concludes that police officers engaged in these race riots actively colluded with white mobs and disproportionately targeted Black suspects for arrest. Similar reports are also published in 1935, 1943, and 1968. (North, 2020) All indicating rampant systemic racism within police forces. All broadly ignored.

This brings us to the present.

As I have illustrated, anti-Blackness is deeply ingrained in the foundation of our country. This history exemplifies how webs of oppression inform our social positionalities and condition our behavior—even today.

Through the lens of Critical Race Theory this history confirms that police brutality is merely one expression of systematized racism. There is a broader deconstruction of institutional racism that must take place first for us to truly dismantle police brutality. Police brutality is a symptom of systemic inequality stemming from our nation's relationship with both capitalism and slavery. Disentangling this systematic discrimination would require an assessment of local governments, financial institutions, zoning laws, and more.

Looking back on the questions I asked at the beginning of this chapter: How is racism systematically embedded in our institutions? How is racism maintained and who benefits from it?

Racism was systemically embedded in our institutions to justify the existence of a racial hierarchy used to exploit Black (and other marginalized groups') labor for profit. Hierarchies of race were created and supported by the scientific community, the government, the criminal justice system, and strict social codes. White hegemony mobilized racial stereotypes to justify stripping away rights from Black communities to mitigate their upward mobility.

Over time, the myths of meritocracy and scarcity—commonly employed in capitalist societies—were used to justify these disparity gaps despite centuries of institutional deprivation that allowed white elites to accumulate wealth and social power at the expense of the Black community. The rhetoric of meritocracy, leaning heavily on the logic of social Darwinism, argues that an individual's social, economic, and political station in life is determined by their ability. Similarly, the myth of scarcity argues that there are a finite number of resources available to satisfy basic human needs, and we often hear rhetoric around the idea of "making hard choices" to justify the uneven distribution of resources in a capitalist society. However, both of these myths are just that—myths.

The reality is the forty acres and a mule newly liberated Black communities were promised as reparations for slavery never materialized due to Lincoln's assassination. (Brown, 2021)

The truth is the Federal Housing Administration (FHA) refused to issue mortgages to Black families in the 1930s, amid a housing shortage, based on the assumption that it would drive property values down. (Gross, 2017) White families were promised newly developed suburban neighborhoods, while Black families were relegated to public housing. (Gross, 2017) These practices laid the groundwork for the racial wealth gap, as the FHA prohibited Black families from buying homes in white suburbs as late as the 1960s. (Gross, 2017)

It is true these racist lending practices stunted Black economic mobility and wealth creation such that Black Americans earn 5 percent the wealth of white Americans. (Gross, 2017)

The reality is housing inequality is compounded by the fact that your zip code determines your access to quality education, health care, and jobs. Housing determines the elections you can vote in, how far your family lives from the waste treatment facility, and the likelihood of having a deadly interaction with law enforcement.

How do you cultivate your abilities without adequate resources? How are resources scarce when our economy can support billionaires but not the millions of people living in poverty? These are the questions individuals are asking now.

Amidst the COVID-19 pandemic, every state and the District of Columbia reached unemployment rates greater than during the Great Recession. (Congressional Research Service, 2021) Forty million Americans filed for unemployment. And yet, "from March to June 2020, Amazon founder Jeff Bezos saw his wealth rise by an estimated $48 billion. The founder of the video-conferencing platform Zoom grew his nest egg by over $2.5 billion, and former Microsoft CEO Steve Ballmer's net worth increased by $15.7 billion." (Woods, 2020)

Across racial, gender, economic, and political lines people took note of this inequity. People who "did the right thing" were suddenly jobless and homeless. And no one is being held responsible for this inequality. Suddenly, the idea that a Black individual could be murdered without consequence becomes more plausible, more infuriating—frankly terrifying for white individuals who did not fully appreciate the severity of these cases before the pandemic.

This interest convergence is powerful. Similar to Bacon's Rebellion, these intersectional solidarities are forcing change amongst white elites out of fear "that the protests against police murders of Black people roiling US cities will transform into a sustained revolt demanding even more radical change." (Morse et al, 2020) Further, "these fears drive the new openness among white elites to truly progressive policies, setting the stage for interest convergence with Black, indigenous, and people of color harmed by underlying structural racism and the unmistakable racial contours of the US pandemic that has been punctuated by horrific murders of Black and Latinx people by police and white terrorists." (Morse et al, 2020)

This is a critical inflection point in United States' history.

We must hold these institutions accountable and face the historical injustices of our nation's past to design a just future. The privileges of a few can no longer be carved out of the oppression of the many.

This is a chance for us all to evaluate our complicity in institutional racism, consider how these oppressive systems work for and against us, and actively invest in designing antiracist solutions.

CHAPTER 6

SUSTAIN THE MOMENTUM

———

We hadn't intended to protest that day. We had planned to pick up dim sum from our favorite hole-in-the-wall in the East Village and sip ice-cold rosé as we caught up on the latest gossip. But there we were, three grown adults with our heads hanging out the window of my friend's black Honda Civic, yelling in unison.

"Black lives matter!" We screamed with joy.

Traffic marshals stopped us at a busy intersection.

We heard them chanting before we saw them—hundreds of protestors chanting, "Hey hey ho ho these racist cops have got to go!" As they streamed past our car, we felt empowered by our collective defiance.

My emotions swung from joy to outrage. Joy to see people of all racial, ethnic, and national backgrounds proudly marching for justice. Enraged that fifty-eight years after Dr. King's March on Washington and fifty-six years after Selma, Black and Brown people are *still* out here marching for our lives.

We shouldn't have to bear this weight, but we do.

I do.

I shouldn't have to watch individuals who look like my family and friends be murdered at the hands of police. It shouldn't be the case that Black people are three times more likely than white people, on average, to be killed during police contact. (Jagannathan, 2020)

I shouldn't have to worry that my parents are going to contract COVID because they are "1.4 times more likely than white persons to develop COVID-19, 3.7 times more likely to be hospitalized with it, and 2.8 times more likely to die from it." (Huizen, 2020) These trends aren't limited to the Black community only—Latinx individuals are 3.7 times more likely to be hospitalized with the virus and 2.8 times more likely to die from it. (Huizen, 2020)

The summer of 2020 we saw colorful protests around the world that made this weight just a little lighter. We saw a global interest and dialogue around systemic racism taking place.

To understand how we capitalize on this momentum and shift from protests to action I interviewed Dr. Robert Patterson, chair of the Department of African American studies at

Georgetown University. Dr. Patterson shared three tactical avenues for effectuating antiracist change.

Defunding the police was first on the list.

Let's set the record straight—defunding the police, when used in the appropriate context, does not mean that we will abandon law enforcement and live in an apocalyptic society. Defunding the police is a reference to Reagan Era legislation which pulled funds from our social safety net to militarize the police in response to the civil rights advances that took place in the 1960s.

It's pretty clear where Reagan stood on the subject of civil rights, and let's just say he was not on the right side of history. The former president opposed the Civil Rights Act of 1964—which prohibited discrimination on the basis of race, color, religion, sex, or national origin—under the guise that this legislation was an infringement on states' rights. (Asante-Muhammad, 2013) He would later attempt to "veto the Civil Rights Restoration Act of 1988, which stipulated that publicly funded institutions had to comply with civil rights laws in all areas of their organization." (Asante-Muhammad, 2013)

In office, Reagan cut funding for a series of social programs leading to disproportionately negative outcomes for Black Americans.

He cut funding for the Equal Employment Opportunity Commission (EEOC) and the civil rights division of the Justice Department—organizations intended to penalize discriminatory practices in education, housing, and the workplace. (Asante-Muhammad, 2013)

He cut government funding for "school lunches, unemployment insurance, childcare, subsidized housing, Aid to Families with Dependent Children (AFDC), and the Comprehensive Employment and Training Act (CETA), which was designed to train workers and enable them to find jobs in the public sector." (Asante-Muhammad, 2013)

These rollbacks reduced social benefit spending by $20 billion a year during a time when Black communities desperately needed these resources to thrive with their newly gained civil rights. (Asante-Muhammad, 2013)

While Reagan extracted this money from social services, he reinvested these funds into militarizing United States police departments.

As Yale historian Elizabeth Hinton highlights, "Reagan stepped into fifteen years of a national crime-control policy that really began—ironically and tragically—at the height of the civil rights revolution, during a time of sweeping liberal reforms." (Guo, 2016) Make no mistake, this crime-control was targeted at one population in particular: the Black community.

Unemployment was high and Black communities were rightfully disgruntled as the promises made in the civil rights period were slowly being rolled back.

Against this backdrop, Reagan's administration called for Congress to pass the Military Cooperation with Civilian

Law Enforcement Agencies Act. This permitted the United States military to collaborate with civilian law enforcement to address the war on drugs. The legislation promoted "the sharing of information and facilities and training on and use of military equipment." (McCabe, 2015)

These policies were strengthened as the bipartisan "war on crime"—a call for a strict criminal justice system—continued to be codified in our legislative system.

George H. W. Bush supported the notable National Defense Authorization Act of 1990 which "authorized the Department of Defense to transfer military equipment to law enforcement agencies 'for use in counter-drug activities' which ultimately led to the Department of Defense Excess Property Program. This program, created under President Bill Clinton, permitted surplus military equipment to be sent to law enforcement agencies for 'use in counternarcotic and counterterrorism operations, and to enhance officer safety.'" (Asante-Muhammad, 2013)

The first step to combatting this unconscionable violence against the Black community is to reinvest the money that has been (inappropriately) used to ramp up police militarization, back into the social safety.

In doing so, money taken from police departments could be funneled back into cities "to build up cities' capacity for crisis care, but also to hire public servants better suited to many of the tasks that consume police officers' time, from dealing with traffic problems to assisting with substance dependency issues." (Collins, 2020) At the same time this reallocation of funds would reduce interactions with the police which would minimize the risk for police misconduct.

Police departments can no longer be used to adjust for market failures where specialized skills are required.

Defunding the police would provide us with the funds to invest in the root causes driving these inequitable outcomes. To make this happen we need representation in all branches of the local, state, and federal government.

This means we have to vote.

When I first asked Dr. Patterson about the connection between COVID-19 and the steep increase in engagement and solidarity around the Black Lives Matter movement, he explained how the outcome of the 2020 election altered his point of view on the link between these events. The strategies Stacey Abrams employed to turn the state of Georgia blue highlight the power of enfranchising first-time, young, Black voters. (King, 2020)

More Americans voted in the November 2020 election than in the past 120 years, as nearly every state saw a record turnout. (Schaul, 2020) Two-thirds of estimated eligible voters participated in the anticipated election casting close to 158.4 million ballots. (Desilver, 2021)

The highly contested battle between incumbent President Donald Trump and contender Joe Biden heightened mounting political stratification as Americans grappled with the day-to-day realities of a health care crisis, racial justice movements, an economic downturn, and the impacts of climate change.

A preelection survey found that 83 percent of registered voters believed it "really mattered" who won. (Desilver, 2021)

Mail balloting and early voting initiatives also played a critical role in expanding voter turnout. According to Pew Research Center, of the ten states with the highest increases in voter turnout rate "seven conducted November's vote entirely or mostly by mail [...] Six of those states had recently adopted all-mail voting, either permanently (Utah and Hawaii) or for the 2020 elections only (California, New Jersey, Vermont and most of Montana)." (Desilver, 2021)

Mail-in ballots decrease the barriers associated with voting, such as transportation costs and lost income, which disproportionately impact communities of color. Removing these barriers can effectively enfranchise these marginalized groups.

Stacey Abrams picked up on this trend before the pandemic.

After losing a tight race against Brian Kemp in 2018, Stacey Abrams hypothesized that "democrats could win more races by expanding their coalition to include disengaged voters of color, as opposed to continuing the focus on persuading undecided, moderate, often white voters." (King, 2020)

In 2020 Abrams got eight hundred thousand voters to register for the election in the state of Georgia, backed by her two organizations: When We Fight and the New Georgia Project.

In doing so, Abrams was able to tip the scales in Georgia, winning Joe Biden the state's electoral college votes and closing the forty-fifth president's chances at winning the election.

Her success offered the Democratic Party a useful blueprint for how to capitalize on shifting demographics and increasing urbanization across the South and highlighted the strength of the Black vote.

Abram's model of community engagement highlights the importance grassroots initiatives can play in driving change on the ground. Her voter registration campaigns are designed for people of color by people of color—the key to developing interventions that disrupt systems of oppression.

One successful model of this community organization—that is close to home for me as a New Yorker—is the Harlem Children's Zone (HCZ). The HCZ is a nonprofit organization that supports education, community outreach, and health and wellness. (Harlem Children's Zone, 2021) The mission of this community-based organization is "to end intergenerational poverty in Central Harlem and lead the way for other long-distressed communities nationwide and around the world to do the same." (Harlem Children's Zone, 2021)

In a TED Talk about the nonprofit, Kwame Owusu-Kesse—their chief executive officer—described the organization as a pioneer in place-based services that offer comprehensive community services from cradle to grave. (TED, 2020) HCZ designs community-driven solutions to combat structural inequalities at the intersections of social institutions such as education, housing, and health care.

By improving environmental conditions and actively dismantling systems of oppression the HCZ has had seven thousand graduates in their "baby college," eliminated the Black-white achievement gap in their schools, reduced obesity rates, and enrolled nearly one thousand students in college. (Harlem Children's Zone, 2021)

With such a comprehensive set of family services, the HCZ is an industry expert on addressing disparities—especially given the devastating impacts of the pandemic.

Owusu-Kesse shares a heart wrenching, and all too familiar, story of one of the HCZ's second grade students named Sean. Owusu-Kesse describes Sean as a "beautiful Black boy whose smile would light up any room that he's in." At the start of the pandemic, Sean stopped attending virtual school because his mom was hospitalized due to COVID-19.

Sean stayed with his grandmother and younger sibling while his mom got better in the hospital. His father was incarcerated, so HCZ was the family's only available support system. His grandma struggled to buy the necessities for Sean and his younger sibling, so buying a computer was certainly off the table. To make matters worse, when Sean's mother was released from the hospital the family was not able to stay with his grandma due to her preexisting conditions, and the family was forced to go to a shelter.

As Sean's story highlights, the accumulated disadvantages experienced by marginalized communities as a result of the pandemic are perpetuated and punctuated by structural inequity.

HCZ provides immediate relief for families in times of crisis by providing a curated list of resources and emergency relief to serve the needs of the community.

This is not a one size fits all solution. The HCZ's community adapted strategies allow the organization to "weave together a net of services so tightly that no one will fall through the cracks." (TED, 2020)

Our government should aspire to this same standard.

PART III

THE POSSIBILITIES

CHAPTER 7

SINK THE SHIPS

If I challenged you to motivate a team to accomplish a daunting task, how would you do it?

If you've read Marcus Buckingham's *The One Thing You Need to Know* you might sit down with every employee to learn their unique strengths. (Lebowitz, 2016)

If you've read Herminia Ibarra's *Act Like a Leader, Think Like a Leader* you may sit back and watch your team fail fast learning from hands-on experience. (Lebowitz, 2016)

If you're a fan of Brené Brown's bestseller *Daring Greatly* you would show vulnerability to show your crew they were safe.

If you've taken a page from the playbook of conquistador Hernán Cortés, however, you might flip the script on "Go big or go home."

Cortés set sail for Mexico with five hundred men, eleven ships, and one obsession: he would defeat the Aztecs. (History, 2019) Not even a direct order to call off the expedition had dissuaded him from pursuing this ambitious mission. As Mexico's shore appeared on the horizon it was time for Cortés to take the helm and issue an order that would surely lead to victory.

He ordered his men to sink ten of their eleven ships, then sent the eleventh back to Spain. (History, 2019)

By destroying their ships, he had left his men with no means to return to Spain. If they lost the battle, they would lose everything. There was no way out and only one path forward: triumph over the Aztecs. They had to win—and they did.

Within the context of a global humanitarian crisis, there are two lessons organizations can learn from the story of Hernán Cortés. First, destroy the ships. Then, once your ships are gone, don't look back.

The ships in the Cortés school of leadership represent the widely held assumptions holding your organization back from innovation. Once your organization has sunk its assumptions with the ship all you can do is lean into the discomfort of operating in the unknown. There's no going back, and the only way out is to chart your own course through radical thinking and innovation.

Challenging these orthodoxies can unlock growth opportunities previously unimaginable. This is how Uber disrupted the taxi market, how Venmo changed the game for consumer payment products, and how Netflix ran Blockbuster out of business. Each company found pockets of opportunity in industries with deeply entrenched operating models.

Start by understanding your customer.

Everyone in a company should be able to speak about their customers as if they were a close friend, a family member, or the neighbor across the street. Frankly, they just might be.

If a company cannot answer the following questions about their consumers, they may not know them at all: What brings them joy? Who do they call for advice? What gets under their skin? What keeps them up at night? What value does your product or service bring to their life? I seriously doubt it is your payroll system.

Based on the year I spent working as a facilitator at an innovation incubator, I do not think many of the executives I worked with could have answered these questions. To be fair, for a long time many of them did not *have* to learn about their consumers at all.

Demographics used to be enough.

But the world has changed. Consumers have changed—they have gotten a lot smarter.

Consumers care about a company's purpose. They care about who made the materials that went into the buttons on their shirt. They care about how many times their jeans were washed during the manufacturing process. They care about the environment, and they care about politics.

They care… and they want the companies they patronize to care about them.

I realized many of the executives I coached on innovation were designing solutions to address their *organization's* challenges rather than addressing their *customer's* challenges. And I think that is the "secret sauce" to innovation.

My former colleague Sana Altaf agreed with this assessment.

Altaf has devoted her career to human-centered design, a structured approach to problem-solving that starts and ends with understanding consumer perspectives. If you are using the approach correctly, she explains, "you're challenging your own assumptions at every step of the way […] because empathy is such a huge component of this methodology, you always have to take a step back and look at [your customer's] problems from different angles."

Innovation is the endless pursuit of expanding the space that connects a company's capabilities to their customer's problems. Innovation is showing customers that you get it. Innovation is that big sigh you let out as a customer when a company makes your life just a little bit easier. It is empathy, as Altaf highlighted.

It took a global pandemic for companies to adopt customer-centric mind-sets. The crisis forced companies to accelerate innovation at an unprecedented rate in response to pandemic-related consumption behaviors that are likely here to stay.

McKinsey & Company—a worldwide management consulting firm—recently published a study that estimated that the COVID-19 pandemic has accelerated the adoption of digital technologies by several years. (LaBerge et al, 2020)

According to the online survey of 899 C-level executives across a range of industries, executives believe their companies have "accelerated the digitization of their customer and supply-chain interactions [...] by three to four years. And the share of digital or digitally enabled products in their portfolios has accelerated by a shocking seven years." (LaBerge et al, 2020)

This acceleration makes sense given the seismic changes in consumer purchasing patterns as a result of the crisis. New shopping behaviors have been formed as consumers are increasingly price sensitive given the state of the global economy. Given this price sensitivity, "value remains the primary reason for consumers to try new brands as well as new places to shop." (Charm et al, 2020)

While consumers are prioritizing value and essentials, they are still taking convenience and availability into consideration when thinking about where to shop; whereas "quality and purpose (desire to support local businesses, for example) are the most important considerations when choosing brands." (Charm et al, 2020)

For companies this translates to an intensely competitive battleground for consumers across industries, segments, and even geographies. With fewer discretionary dollars on the table, it is not just about convincing customers that you have the best product; it is justifying that they should even buy a product in the first place.

Companies are innovating for survival. There is simply no other option. There is a phrase for that—necessity is the mother of invention. But who says you can't create your own necessity?

The rapidly evolving business environment forced companies to sink their ships. Going digital was no longer a luxury but a requirement to keep the lights on. Contactless transactions were not just a perk but a critical safety precaution.

The pandemic unleashed a wave of global innovation at a rate unimaginable just one year ago. People have changed the way they work, the way they shop, how they spend their free time, and how they connect with friends. Through crisis consumers have revealed how adaptable they are. And, against all odds, successful corporations have done the same.

Take a luxury fashion and perfume company, a British technology company, and a multinational retailer for example. Pre-pandemic these companies had little in common, but at the outset of the crisis they each quickly adapted their business models to address immediate consumer needs.

Four days after the World Health Organization declared that the coronavirus outbreak was classified as a pandemic, the luxury goods conglomerate LVMH announced that three of their perfume manufacturing facilities would be converted to produce hand sanitizer for the French government at no cost. (Kestenbaum, 2020) Just a few weeks later Dyson Limited, prominent for their vacuum cleaners, would publicize that in record time they were able to design, build, and manufacture the Dyson CoVent. Configured to meet the specialized needs of coronavirus patients, the CoVent was created to address the global shortage in ventilators. (Bashir, 2020) In

September of 2020 Walmart Inc. forged partnerships with three drone companies to prototype grocery and COVID-19 test delivery straight to their customer's door. (Cain, 2020)

These companies efficiently expanded business operations to address the immediate needs of their customers and communities. I call this strategy of innovation *expanding the core*, as these companies broadened the scope of services provided to their consumers by exploring new opportunities to capitalize on their market expertise.

By doubling down on their core capabilities, these organizations used this innovation strategy to redefine their value proposition for consumers and to develop new products and services with the potential to organically grow their businesses. I challenge companies taking this approach to innovation to consider how they can continue to innovate at this rate following the crisis.

Rather than returning to normal, these companies must carefully evaluate the capabilities they have unlocked during the pandemic. What other alcohol-based solutions or products could LVMH produce? How could Dyson redesign their research and development process to develop new airflow solutions at record pace? How might Walmart completely redesign the consumer shopping and delivery process with drones?

By evaluating the orthodoxies that the pandemic has debunked, these companies can continue to drive disruptive innovations that are relevant beyond the current environment.

Some companies took the core expansion route to innovation, but I also noticed another group of companies taking a more drastic approach. For these companies the pandemic seems to be an opportunity to reshape their operating model such that they are *optimizing the core* to enable long-term efficiencies. A key feature of this approach is a strategic investment in technology.

For example, Chinese e-commerce giant Alibaba Group has launched a smart hotel concept in their FlyZoo Hotel. These unmanned hotels allow guests to "book a room and do check in online using facial recognition, turn out the lights, draw the curtains or adjust the air conditioner, all without human assistance." (Reeves et al, 2020) All of this is made possible by Alibaba's heavy investment in artificial intelligence and Internet of Things technology which enables seamless connection to the internet across these devices.

Similarly, Chinese cosmetics company Lin Qingxuan redeployed over one hundred of their beauty advisors from closed stores to digital platforms, such as WeChat, to drive sales and engage customers directly. (Reeves et al, 2020) This direct-to-consumer strategy translated to 200 percent sales growth compared to the prior year's sales in Wuhan—the city that was cut off from the rest of China when it was identified as the epicenter of the virus. (Reeves et al, 2020) That's right, Lin Qingxuan was able to achieve double their sales growth by empowering their beauty advisors to become social media influencers.

While both of these strategies could have been executed pre-pandemic, it seems something transformative has been unlocked in these companies due to the crisis. By optimizing their core capabilities these companies created more relevant offerings for their consumer base.

Unlike core expansion, these organizations are not creating new products and services. Instead, they are refining their operating model to enhance the customer experience. This customer centric approach establishes new touch points for engaging with consumers. New touch points mean rich data sets which can then be analyzed to continually create meaningful interactions that drive value.

As I read more about companies expanding and optimizing their core business, I wondered if there were any companies with a more proactive strategy. Were there any companies that saw consumer behavior shifting and reacted accordingly?

One example in China stood out.

Master Kong—the largest instant noodle producer in China—anticipated hoarding and stock-outs at the onset of the virus and was able to shift their fulfillment priorities from offline to online channels. By monitoring retail outlets' reopening plans, Master Kong was able to dynamically adjust their supply chain to respond to trends in demand. It turns out this responsiveness created a huge competitive advantage, as a few weeks following the outbreak "[Master Kong's] supply chain had recovered by more than 50 percent […] and it was able to supply 60 percent of the stores that were reopened during this period—three times as many as some competitors." (Reeves et al, 2020)

Why? I say because they have a *predictive core*. Taking innovation a step further, Master Kong's regular analysis of reopening plans enabled the company to predict consumer needs and respond proactively in light of that data.

This strategy, compared to the other two approaches, is much more proactive. Master Kong did not have to wait to see how the pandemic unfolded to put this strategy in place. They calibrated their response based on predictive signals.

Companies with a predictive core are well positioned for rapid innovation for two key reasons.

First, as the name suggests, they are able to make sense of customer trends in real time. Seems easy, right? Wrong. It's *easy* to realize that your consumers are buying more of your product. It is much more difficult, however, to identify hoarding behavior and then learn to anticipate that behavior based on retail reopening strategies.

The latter requires an intimate understanding of your consumer base and the forces that impact their buying decision. Now that's value.

But it's about more than just unlocking the right insights. Companies also have to have the organizational agility to quickly act on this information. And if this pandemic has taught us anything it's that you have to be agile. From your company culture to supply chain operations, embedding agility must be a strategic priority to withstand this pandemic—and the next one.

So what characteristics are markers of success in this landscape? Looking across these examples, I see a relentless focus on evolving consumer needs. Every decision must be made to support a strategy that provides value to your consumers. Supporting these customer-centric strategies are digital initiatives. Due to the nature of the virus companies can no longer rely on physical touch points with their consumers, employees, and suppliers to drive value. Instead, digital solutions have been used to create rich virtual environments to maintain engagement and connect with key stakeholders.

The data supports this. "At the organizations that experimented with new digital technologies during the crisis, and among those that invested more capital expenditures in digital technology than their peers did, executives are twice as likely to report [outsized] revenue growth than executives at other companies," McKinsey & Company reported. (LaBerge et al, 2020) The companies that are placing big bets on digital strategies are also reaping massive rewards, which is the perfect segue to the last ingredient for success in this environment—experimentation.

Research suggests that companies who are first movers in experimenting with new digital technologies and first to market with innovations during the crisis have a competitive advantage. (LaBerge et al, 2020) As the economic and humanitarian crises continues to unfold, experimentation and prototyping are imperative to act quickly and remain proactive as consumer preferences and consumption habits evolve. I know rapid prototyping often gets a bad rap, but the proof is in the pudding when it comes to the results.

Believe me, I understand the instinct to hoard knowledge and only share ideas once they have been fully developed and completely defined in an epic PowerPoint deck that has been signed off by your manager and their manager and so on. But why put in all that work without the input of your consumers?

While it might be intimidating at first, it is more valuable to get feedback from key stakeholders along the way to ensure your final deliverable is desirable for the end-user, technologically feasible, and fundamentally viable for your business. Therein lies the power of prototyping. By gathering input along the way, you are able to address the feedback you receive iteratively *as* you develop your product rather than redesigning or reworking a fully developed concept.

Ultimately, successful companies that foster a culture of innovation and experimentation "are more likely than others to report speeding up the time it takes for leaders to receive critical business information and reallocating resources to fund new initiatives." (LaBerge et al, 2020) These companies are optimally positioned to act quickly to respond to changing market forces and consumer needs.

The ball lies in each company's court. This is a critical turning point for every business—regardless of industry, specialty, or consumer base. It's time for companies to take inventory of the lessons they have learned and the capabilities they have unlocked since the onset of the virus. In a post-COVID society, companies must evaluate how business models should continue to evolve to take advantage of this newly realized potential.

How might a company innovate if COVID-19 was predominantly airborne and none of us could leave our homes? How would consumer behavior change if the symptomology associated with COVID-19 was more severe?

These are the orthodoxies companies must challenge once the behaviors associated with the current operating model become the norm.

***

The unprecedented circumstances surrounding the COVID-19 pandemic have forced companies to innovate for survival. However, it should not have taken a crisis to activate this newfound focus on customer centricity, corporate responsibility, and innovation. To remain competitive in this environment companies must quickly adopt current ways of working as the new normal and develop human-centered solutions to solve the problems tomorrow may bring.

And what choice do companies have? Their ships have already been destroyed.

CHAPTER 8

WE CAN'T STOP
THE CLOCK

The clock is ticking.

For 650 years, ornate rice paddy terraces have cascaded across China's sprawling hillsides, carving out iconic monuments to man's power to manipulate nature. Now barren fields scar the once lush landscape in Hunan province, where nature has deprived villagers of the one thing they need most for the cultivation of rice—water.

The sea once brought prosperity to the palm-lined shores of Ada Foah, Ghana. Golden sands lined the coast of the estuary where the Volta River and Atlantic Ocean converge, and the villagers welcomed tourists and traders to the bustling oasis. Now the community retreats as the violent tides bury their homes and businesses under mounds of sand. The water took everything it brought.

A violent wildfire in Manitou Springs, Colorado, took two lives and destroyed 347 homes, leaving nineteen thousand acres of forest burnt in its wake. (Deam, 2020) A year later the aftermath of this natural disaster would continue to wreak havoc in the city when seasonal rainfall created an "avalanche of water" that otherwise would have been absorbed by the lush forest. (Deam, 2020) One resident of the area described feeling like "it's just one disaster to the next" for this resort city in Colorado, renowned for its mineral springs and mountainous landscapes. (Climate Reality, 2013)

We don't often know what the future will hold, but with the climate we have a pretty good idea.

Droughts. Rising sea levels. Wildfires. Floods. This will be our future if we do not mitigate the lethal impacts of climate change.

The time we have to limit climate change is running out.

We do not have much time to ensure global warming stays under the 1.5°C threshold. We do not have much time to grow the world's supply of renewable energy from 28.12 percent to 100 percent. ("The Climate Clock", 2021) We do not have much time to prevent the estimated fifty-four trillion dollars' worth of damage expected by 2040. (DiChristopher, 2019)

We do not have much time to save the world.

The COVID-19 pandemic has offered an unsettling glimpse into our future. As temperatures continue to rise our climate will become more humid and create the ideal environment for pathogens to grow and for bacteria-carrying species, like mosquitos, to thrive. (Climate Reality Project, 2019).

My former colleague Maggie Kervick works as a corporate impact consultant to Fortune 500 clients. I asked Kervick to share her perspective on the connection between climate change and COVID-19, and her sobering warning sent a chill down my spine.

"COVID-19 is the dress rehearsal for what is to come with climate change."

Let's take a step back.

Global warming is caused by humans burning fossil fuels to create energy. Over millions of years buried remnants of plants and animals pressed deeper and deeper into the ground forming these byproducts. (Smithsonian, 2020) As pressure and heat builds around these remains they decompose and are transformed into natural gas, oil, and coal. (Smithsonian, 2020)

Today businesses and individuals extract fossilized plants from the earth through the processes of mining for coal and drilling for oil. These burned fossil fuels are then processed and used to power machinery, transportation, and electricity. (McFall-Johnsen, 2019)

These burning fossil fuels trap heat in our atmosphere—emitting large quantities of carbon dioxide into the environment, which ultimately cause changes in our climate. (Denchak, 2020)

Scientists estimate these ecological changes will reach a peak when global warming meets or exceeds 1.5°C.

Within the United Nations, the task of developing ongoing scientific assessments on climate change falls on the Intergovernmental Panel on Climate Change (IPCC). In its 2019 assessment the IPCC reported that if global warming exceeded the 1.5°C threshold "several regional changes in climate […] compared to pre-industrial levels, including warming of extreme temperatures in many regions" would take place. (Masson-Delmotte et al, 2018)

To address the immediate need for change, the Paris Agreement was developed in December of 2015 and adopted by 196 parties. The Paris Agreement is a legally binding international treaty with the goal of "[limiting] global warming to well below 2, preferably to 1.5 degrees Celsius, compared to pre-industrial levels." (United Nations, 2021) The treaty represents a landmark in multilateral climate change action as it was the first time a binding agreement was developed to hold nations accountable for combatting climate change.

Despite these efforts, the same IPCC report concluded these actions will not be drastic enough.

[With] emissions in line with current pledges under the Paris Agreement (known as Nationally Determined Contributions, or NDCs), global warming is expected to surpass 1.5°C above pre-industrial levels, even if these pledges are supplemented with very challenging [increases] in the scale and ambition of mitigation after 2030. (Rogelj et al, 2018)

We are already seeing some of the dire impacts of human-induced global warming today.

As greenhouse gases trap excess heat in our atmosphere, different parts of the planet absorb and reflect light at different rates. In the Central Arctic dark ocean water absorbs more than 90 percent of sunlight and the white ice covering it absorbs between 30 to 40 percent. (Fountain, 2020)

The dark water attracts more heat which causes the ice on top of the ocean to melt. As this ice melts the surface area of the ocean becomes even more exposed to the sunlight— in turn attracting more heat and melting more ice.

Emerging science suggests the impacts of Arctic warming have the power to alter the polar jet stream—high-altitude winds which bring winter weather to North America and Europe—by creating zones of high-pressure air with the power to alter weather patterns across the Northern Hemisphere. (Fountain, 2020)

In the Himalayan region the steep increase in temperatures has had disastrous consequences for the surrounding communities.

Permafrost melts from glaciers and "weather patterns are becoming more erratic, disrupting previously reliable water sources for millions and instigating more natural disasters." (Borunda, 2019) For the 240 million people that call this region home, this means droughts and floods caused by the changing patterns of snow and rain. This results in weaker monsoons, "starving the mountains of the snow that feeds glaciers and that provides key water to many farmers as it slowly melts through the springtime, right when they need water to get their crops planted." (Borunda, 2019) Glacial lakes have more than doubled since 1977 increasing the risk that they will burst through rock piles, due to their weight, and lead to devastating floods. (Borunda, 2019) Therefore, collapsing terrains and avalanches will become common-place in the region. (Borunda, 2019)

These diverse risks increase the frequency of disasters and the likelihood that they will worsen as the region's temperatures continue to rise.

The ocean's surface continues to warm, and natural disasters like hurricanes will increase in intensity.

Scientists have discovered that for each degree Fahrenheit of warming, there is a correlated ten-mile-per-hour increase in sustained peak winds in Category 5-level storms. For reference, a 7 percent increase in wind speed translates to a 20 percent approximate increase in the maximum intensity of the hurricane. (Climate Reality Project, 2017)

We have seen these impacts in action. "When global sea surface temperatures have been at their highest, we have seen the strongest hurricane globally, the strongest hurricane in the Northern Hemisphere, the strongest hurricane in the Southern Hemisphere, and the strongest storms in both the Pacific and the open Atlantic, with Irma." (Climate Reality Project, 2017)

Climatologists caution higher temperatures will lead to more precipitation falling in the form of rain rather than snow, and this will cause earlier snowmelt and increased rates of evaporation and transpiration. As temperatures rise so too does the risk of hydrological and agricultural drought. ("Causes of Drought: What's the Climate Connection?", 2014) The Natural Resources Defense Council (NRDC), a United States-based international environmental advocacy group, found that the "drought conditions jeopardize access to clean drinking water, fuel out-of-control wildfires, and result in dust storms, extreme heat events, and flash flooding in the States." (Denchak, 2016)

Atmospheric moisture increases and rainfall grows heavier. That water must go somewhere, and so it runs off into streams, rivers, and lakes. When those bodies can't handle the increasing volume of water they overflow. The unfiltered water has the potential to contaminate our drinking water, create hazardous material spills, and significantly diminish our air quality. (Denchak, 2016)

Rising sea levels also threaten our ecological systems.

A study published by the *Proceedings of the National Academy of Sciences of the United States of America (PNAS)* found that the Greenland Ice Sheet started losing mass balance outside of normal seasonal variability in the 1980s. (Jérémie et al, 2019) At equilibrium the melting that occurs during warm cycles should counteract the new ice formed during the cooler cycles. As a result of global warming, however, the ice melted during the warmer months is not regenerated by new ice in the cooler months—leading to a decrease in the ice sheet's mass.

The researchers who developed this study reconstructed the mass balance of the Greenland Ice Sheet for the past forty-six years and found that "the mass loss has increased six-fold since the 1980s." (Mouginot et al, 2019) Ultimately, this has raised the sea level by 13.7 mm since 1972, half of which occurred during the last eight years. (Mouginot et al, 2019) Additionally—according to the United States National Climate Assessment—by 2030 this could lead to an average 0.3–0.6 feet of sea level rise.

High tide flooding also threatens communities on the United States Gulf Coast and East Coast. By 2030 "projections suggest the [U.S. Northeast] will see a median of five floods per year. By 2045, that number could grow to 25 floods." (McFall-Johnsen, 2019) Rising sea levels are already impacting low-lying cities like Miami, New Orleans, Venice, Jakarta, and Lagos. (McFall-Johnsen, 2019) Some estimates project sea levels to get up to six feet higher by the end of the century. (McFall-Johnsen, 2019)

Remember back in third-grade science class when you learned that warm water takes up more volume than colder water? As it turns out, the same principle of physics applies to our oceans—as ocean temperatures rise seas rise too. Scientists expect this phenomenon to account for roughly 75 percent of future sea level rise. (McFall-Johnsen, 2019)

These abrupt changes to weather patterns and the composition of our marine ecosystem will have dire consequences on our global food supply.

According to a special report on food security issued by the IPCC, "Observed climate change is already affecting food security through increasing temperatures, changing precipitation patterns, and greater frequency of some extreme events." (Mbow et al, 2019)

In Australia declining rainfalls and increasing daily maximum temperatures caused water-limited yield potential to decline by 27 percent from 1990 to 2015, even while elevated atmospheric carbon dioxide concentrations had a positive effect. (Mbow et al, 2019) Crop yield studies focusing on India have found that warming has reduced wheat yields by 5.2 percent from 1981 to 2009, despite efforts to adapt to these conditions. (Mbow et al, 2019) In 2019 the United Nations launched an international campaign for $234 million in emergency aid for Zimbabwe where drought is expected to affect a third of the country's crop and leave 5.3 million people requiring aid. (Ndlovu, 2019)

Many of these risks to global food supply will be exacerbated by nonenvironmental stressors as well.

Over the past sixty years food supply per capita has increased more than 30 percent "accompanied by greater use of nitrogen fertilizers (increase of about 800 percent) and water resources for irrigation (increase of more than 100 percent)." (Mbow et al, 2019) From this vantage point, climate change will only place additional pressures on a food system that is already overextended. (Mbow et al, 2019)

Global crop and economic models project a 1–29 percent cereal price increase by 2050 due to climate change. 1–183 million additional people will be at risk of hunger. (Mbow et al, 2019) Distributions of pests and diseases will change with negative outcomes impacting many regions. (Mbow et al, 2019) These projections suggest that "given increasing extreme events and interconnectedness, risks of food system disruptions are growing." (Mbow et al, 2019)

Combined, the effects of climate change have severe implications for public health.

Remember that melting permafrost I was talking about? Well, as the permafrost melts it releases "ancient microbes that today's humans have never been exposed to—and as a result have no resistance to." (Figueres et al, 2020) On top of that, species like mosquitoes and ticks will thrive in our new, humid climate and will spread disease across the planet in ways we have never seen before. The current public health crisis of antibiotic resistance—stemming from our overuse of antibiotics and general lack of infection prevention and control measures—will escalate and continue to be perpetuated by population growth and global warming. Our vital resources—food and water—will also be threatened, as this intense climate will give rise to food and waterborne illnesses that will diminish population health and heighten our food insecurity.

The founders of Global Optimism, Christiana Figueres—former executive secretary of the United Nations Framework Convention on Climate Change—and Tom Rivett-Carnac, wrote a book on what our world would actually look like if temperatures surpassed the 1.5°C threshold.

In *The Future We Choose: Surviving the Climate Crisis*, Figueres and Rivett-Carnac describe two futures for our world: one where we act to halve emissions this decade, and the other where we continue on our current path and fail.

The future they describe is terrifying.

Surface ozone levels created a humid climate where air quality is so degraded that we have to check our phones to determine if it is safe to go outside. (Figueres et al, 42) Extreme weather forces mass evacuations, as the moisture in the air combined with the higher sea surface temperatures make hurricanes and tropical storms more frequent and catastrophic. Aid organizations scramble to provide displaced communities with access to resources.

Several places around the world are becoming uninhabitable due to the sweltering heat causing droughts and the rising sea levels causing floods. This leads to "mass migrations to less hot rural areas [which] are beset by a host of refugee problems, civil unrest, and bloodshed over diminished water availability." (Figueres et al, 2020)

Conflict is not just something you watch on the news—it is ingrained in everyday life. Global trade is slower as countries are forced to hoard resources for communities in need.

As Figueres and Rivett-Carnac state, "disasters and wars rage, choking off trade routes. The tyranny of supply and demand is now unforgiving, food can now be wildly expensive. Income inequality has never been this stark or this dangerous." (Figueres et al, 2020)

This is the reality we are creating. We have to wise up.

We need to shift our mind-sets. Figueres and Rivett-Carnac describe three mind-sets we need to adopt if we are going to undertake the monumental task of slowing down climate change. I have provided short mantras for each, and I encourage you all to use these to remember that even one person can make a difference.

The first is Stubborn Optimism. The mantra for this mind-set is "I am not helpless. I can make a difference. I will make a difference that will impact generations to come." This mind-set describes an intentional focus and commitment to slowing the rate of global warming, despite how daunting this may seem.

There is hope.

Figueres and Rivett-Carnac offset their somber prediction with hints of optimism. "When your mind tells you that it will be impossible for the world to lighten its dependence on fossil fuels, remember that already more than 50 percent of the energy in the UK comes from clean power, that Costa Rica is 100 percent clean, and that California has a plan to get 100 percent clean, including cars and trucks, by the time today's toddlers have finished college." (Figueres et al, 90)

The second mind-set shift is Endless Abundance. Scarcity is a myth employed to support the inequitable outcomes of capitalism. I often hear the myth of scarcity invoked when people say things like, "We have to make tough choices," or, "We all have to make sacrifices." These are falsities perpetuated by a capitalist economic agenda.

But COVID-19 has shown us scarcity does not need to be our reality.

In the United States pharmaceutical organizations have created lifesaving vaccines that have been administered to vulnerable populations at no cost. During this pandemic we have created new channels and methods for delivering vital resources to individuals in need. We have shared our knowledge with other nations so we may collectively fight this virus. And we do not have to stop here.

By adopting this mind-set of Endless Abundance, we can break out of the psychological hold of scarcity and focus our efforts on a common purpose. We can break out of this zero-sum paradigm whereby we feel that someone else's gain comes at a loss to ourselves. The authors explain, "the practice of abundance starts by shifting our minds away from perceived scarcity to what we can collectively *make* abundant. In so doing, we will become more aware of others, what we can learn from them and share with them." (Figueres et al, 125)

Say this mantra when you need a reminder that there are more than enough resources to go around: "I can receive as much as I give."

The last mind-set is Radical Regeneration. This describes the necessity for us to radically reinvent our relationship with the planet—the reality is our environment can no longer support the ways in which humans have organized their life on earth.

"Instead of strip-mined mountains, destroyed forests, and depleted oceans, imagine millions of re-wilding projects covering over a billion hectares of forests, regenerating wetlands and grasslands, and restoring coral farms in all tropical oceans," the authors suggest. (Figueres et al, 141)

Through innovation we can design for regeneration. We can recreate the way we think about energy, the way we think about water conservation, and the way we think about transportation so that we are not simply taking away from our planet—but restoring it. So that we can be sustainable *and* productive. So that we can create value for people over the long term.

The mantra for this mind-set is simple, "I will choose the planet. The choices I make will allow life on earth to thrive."

Along with these mind-sets, we need to make some pretty tangible changes—and quickly.

Surviving the climate crisis requires an overhaul of the systems and institutions that got us here in the first place.

Quick wins will not save us.

We need to decarbonize the energy supply that has accumulated in the environment. (Rogelj et al, 2018) We need to use smart grids and technologies that optimize our energy storage to limit warming. (Rogelj et al, 2018) We need to offset the excess carbon in the environment by supporting oxygenation initiatives to filter out polluted air. We need to optimize our use of renewable sources. We need to reduce our transportation needs. We need to normalize plant-based alternatives and stop relying on energy-depleting food sources. We need global cooperation to share knowledge and design innovative solutions.

To make this reality feasible, we must first acknowledge the problem exists and then develop human-centered solutions that benefit communities and restore our environment.

We can't stop the clock, but we can change what happens before the timer runs out.

CHAPTER 9

FLIP THE SCRIPT

Is capitalism bullshit?

If your last name isn't Bezos, Musk, or Zuckerberg then it very well may be. Our industrialized brand of capitalism is not designed to serve the needs of the common person.

Trevor Hill, a charismatic New York University student, wondered what alternative economic models were available. During a CNN Town Hall, Hill wanted answers.

In response to former President Donald Trump's astounding victory against Hillary Clinton, CNN held a Town Hall with House Minority Leader Nancy Pelosi to discuss Democratic strategies for resisting the Republican triumph. (Sainato, 2017)

CNN producers rejected Hill's question during preplanning discussions, instructing the student to pose a simple, personal question for Congresswoman Pelosi. Hill tacitly agreed but chose to ask his question anyway. (Seipel, 2017)

"I wonder if there's anywhere you feel the Democrats could move farther left to a more populist message the way the alt-right has sort of captured this populist strain on the right wing, if you think we could make a more stark contrast to right-wing economics?" he asked. (Sainato, 2017)

Caught off guard, perhaps, by such an existential question the seasoned politician retorted, "I thank you for your question, but I'm sorry to say we're capitalists, and that's just the way it is." (CNN, 2017) Pelosi went on to explain how the wealth gap has been widened by the shift from stakeholder to shareholder capitalism that has occurred over the past twenty years. (CNN, 2017)

She described stakeholder capitalism as a time when business operators made strategic decisions by considering the impact to their customers, employees, and shareholders. (CNN, 2017) Shareholder capitalism is strictly concerned with increasing the bottom line to return back to owners of the company. (CNN, 2017)

To correct and discourage shareholder capitalism, simply "change the thinking of people," she recommended. (Sainato, 2017) If only it were that simple.

***

The pandemic unlocked dissatisfaction with the American economic system. Policies previously dismissed as radical or impractical shifted to the foreground of the government's pandemic response.

At a cost to taxpayers of $5.3 trillion, the first six COVID-19 relief bills included provisions to subsidize salaries, administer aid to small businesses, provide rental and mortgage assistance, send direct aid to state, local, and tribal governments, extend unemployment benefits, fund vaccine distribution and testing services, strengthen mental health services, bolster educational support, and more. (Peter G Peterson Foundation, 2021)

As the economy crashed, so too did consumer confidence in capitalism. Among Gen Z adults 54 percent reported espousing negative views of capitalism, according to polling. (Manchester, 2021) Can you blame them? It is hard to support a profit-driven economic model in the midst of a humanitarian crisis.

After years of unencumbered economic growth, the pandemic shut our economy down in a matter of weeks. Unemployment jumped to 14.7 percent by April 2020—the highest we had seen in the post–World War II era. (Patton, 2020) Consumer spending plummeted to the lowest level since 1932. As a result, "gross domestic product decreased 3.5 percent in 2020, the biggest drop since 1946. That followed 2.2 percent growth in 2019 and was the first annual decline in GDP since the 2007–09 Great Recession." (Mutikani, 2021)

Capitalism is not the problem. Our government failing to regulate how corporate profit translates to consumer value— that is the problem.

Economist Mariana Mazzucato has dedicated her career to investigating where and how we drifted off course quantifying and debating how institutions create value for consumers. Over the past three hundred years, Mazzucato argues, a philosophical shift has taken place. (TED, 2019)

At one point, she explains, we had it right.

Back when our economy was based on agricultural production, economists rigorously audited how specific roles contributed to value creation. (TED, 2019) To do this, these economists used a tool called the Tableau économique to simulate how value was created and transferred through the process of farming. The intricate diagram segmented the workforce into three classes: the productive class, the proprietors, and the sterile class.

Farmers created value by producing commodities that could be sold on the free market—this made them the productive class. Proprietors, or merchants, supported the agrarian economy by transporting goods from the farm to the buyers, serving as necessary middlemen between the productive class and consumers. Landowners were considered sterile because they charged farmers a fee to use their land.

Early theorists believed the sterile class posed a monumental risk to the economic system. While the sterile class received profits from the agrarian process, they did not create value. The Tableau économique modeled "what would actually happen under different scenarios if the wealth [...] wasn't reinvested back into production to make that land more productive and was actually being siphoned out in different ways," Mazzucato explains. (TED, 2019) To monitor this production activity, economists traced where wealth was derived, how it was exchanged across classes, and the percentage of wealth that was reinvested back into production activities. (Mazzucato, 31)

Theories of value creation remained heavily contested as our economy shifted from agrarian to industrial. Rather than analyze value exchanges in agricultural production, philosophers like Adam Smith and Karl Marx focused on the relationship between labor and productivity.

Just as economists of the past documented in the Tableau économique, Smith categorized income from industrial labor into discrete categories. He concluded that individuals who profited from renting their land to producers were siphoning value out of the economy. Smith referred to this method of wealth creation as rent-seeking behavior, as wealth was being created without a reciprocal investment into productivity. In Smith's conception of the free-market economy he called for limitation of this form of income he deemed exploitive. (Mazzucato, 40)

A generation later, Karl Marx ultimately criticized how capitalism creates and perpetuates class stratification. Marx noticed a shift in power dynamics as industrialization spread. He noticed that ordinary people could no longer independently produce goods. Members of the working class no longer owned land and therefore no longer had a means to produce their own food. Their dependence on funds for the purchase of sustenance rendered them reliant on compensation for their labor. (TED, 2019) The working class were, determined Marx, wholly dependent on capitalists.

Under the previous economic structure the average person owned the profits of their surplus crop. However, in the industrial environment workers received compensation for the time and effort required to produce a surplus but retained no rights to that surplus. This is an inherently exploitive relationship.

These shifting power dynamics would set the stage for new methods of exploitation in the name of profit. The institution of slavery "opened the arteries of capital and commerce that led to U.S. economic dominance worldwide." (Baradaran, 10)

Think about that for a second. The United States commoditized human bodies to increase production capacity and codified a racial hierarchy to justify this rent-seeking behavior. That is how we lost our way. Enslaved men, women, and children were forced to create value in an economy they could never participate in.

We conflated price with value. We traded humanity for profit.

We shifted our attention from how value is created and extracted to how price impacts demand and supply. (TED, 2019) This new branch of economics, known as neoclassicism, assumes corporations set the maximum price for their products and consumers purchase these products at a price that maximizes their happiness. (TED, 2019) Price, rather than the dynamics driving production activities, became the mechanism we used to understand and assess value.

Converging price and value made gross domestic product an attractive quantitative measurement for economic output.

GDP represents the total market value, or price, of all finished goods and services produced in a country over a specific period of time. (Fernando, 2021) A UK Treasury official created the calculation in 1940 to quantify Britain's ability to mobilize capacity during World War II. To solve this problem, he took matters into his own hands and estimated national income could be calculated by summing private consumption, investment, and government spending. (Kapoor et al, 2019) While this measurement certainly met Britain's needs during the war, it is still used today to assess economic growth and development.

As Mazzucato warns, this measurement is limited because it does not quantify the positive or negative impacts associated with the process of production and development.

GDP takes stock of the number of cars we produce but does not adjust for the emissions they emit into our environment. GDP accounts for the salaries the government pays to public school teachers, but not the value that is extracted when children receive this education. GDP highlights government spending on the health care system, but not the value of a healthy national population.

"If you marry your babysitter, GDP will go down, so do not do it [...]. Because an activity that perhaps was before being paid for is still being done but is no longer paid," Mazzucato remarks playfully. (TED, 2019) On the other end of the spectrum, GDP increases when we emit carbon into the environment because "then we have to pay someone to clean it." (TED, 2019)

How can the government manage and control for market failures if the very metrics used to measure our performance as a nation are out of whack? So out of whack that our GDP is bolstered by negative climate action and dampened by education expenditures.

How can we build wealth if the government does not manage rent-seeking behavior? Rent-seeking behavior that causes hardworking families to struggle for survival, while billionaires are able to extract colossal profits without directly contributing to value creating activities.

These power dynamics are heightened during times of crisis.

If COVID-19 taught us anything, it is that we have to reimagine the foundations of our economic system to mitigate the excessive burden market failures can place on our vulnerable populations.

The government has to recognize where value is created and extracted in our current socioeconomic atmosphere. Our policies must disincentivize rent-seeking behavior. Our economists must be challenged to redefine how we quantify and track consumer happiness, the negative impacts of climate change, racial injustice, and inadequate health care.

The bottom line is the government has to have some skin in the game and work closely with the private sector to stimulate innovation in areas of our economy that produce the greatest value to our consumers.

Value starts and ends with us. It's about time we flip the script and set the terms for a new capitalism.

PART IV

CONCLUSION

CHAPTER 10

IT TOOK A CRISIS

———

Joseph Palma had a good job. The income he earned as a United States Border and Customs agent at the Miami International Airport would never make him a rich man, but it was steady. (Tavernise et al, 2020) When the CDC diagnosed the first case of coronavirus in Washington State in January 2020, Palma had no idea how drastically it would impact his life—or how quickly.

One day after the first COVID-19 case appeared within our borders the federal government began shutting down international air travel—slowly at first, then all at once. That spring, airlines and airports furloughed and laid off tens of thousands of workers. And then it happened. At forty-one, Palma was unemployed and living with his mother again. (Tavernise et al, 2020) Without a severance package to cushion the blow of an unexpected job loss, he knew his $3,100 bank account balance wouldn't last long. (Tavernise et al, 2020) It wouldn't begin to make a dent in the $15,000 medical debt coming his way after two hospital stays. (Tavernise et al, 2020) "I don't know what's the ending," he said, "but I know I'm not in good shape." (Tavernise et al, 2020) Drowning and desperate, Palma reached for a lifeline. But the unemployment office's phone lines and website were overwhelmed—he could not get through. If help was out there, he couldn't access it.

Yvette Beatty is the matriarch and sole provider for her family of seven. (Kinder et al, 2020) Her health wasn't great, but she couldn't afford to slow down. (Kinder et al, 2020) Some months she couldn't even afford to take her medication the way she was supposed to—she skipped a dose here and there to stretch the time between refills. (Kinder et al, 2020) "It's very hard," she said. "Thank God for noodles. We are just eating what we can right now." (Kinder et al, 2020) When Mayor Jim Kenney issued Philadelphia's first stay-at-home order in March 2020, Beatty knew her health problems put her in the COVID-19 high risk category, but she couldn't afford to stay home, and she didn't have to. More than seven million older Americans depend on home care providers like Beatty—her job was essential to her clients and their families, and Beatty's $12.75 per hour paycheck was essential to her own. (Allison et al, 2020; Kinder et al, 2020)

Olivia Fernandes and her husband Fabio built a life for themselves in Miami. The young fitness instructors brought in $77,000 a year—slightly above the median income for Miami-Dade County. (Miami Dade Matters, 2021) They were comfortable. After three years of marriage, Mrs. Fernandes still hadn't met her in-laws in person. It was time for a vacation—they eagerly planned their first trip to visit Mr. Fernandes's parents. Life was good until the mayor shut down gyms on March 17, 2020. (Hanks et al, 2021) With no income they regretted having used their savings to pay down their student loan debt. The end of the month crept closer. Rent was due—no exceptions. Student loan payments piled up. By April 2020 they would have very little to their name. The two looked at each other and said, "Oh my god, we have lost it all." (Tavernise et al, 2020)

For many Americans the pandemic has been characterized by loss. Loss of health insurance, job security, or even a loved one. The year reminded us that we are all one checkup, one paycheck, or one phone call away from losing it all. That is how crises unfold—at first slowly, then all at once.

We collected loss while the ultra-rich collected profit. America's 664 billionaires accumulated $1.62 trillion of wealth between March 2020 and April 2021. (Kaplan, 2021) Approximately every seventeen hours, from March 2020 to March 2021, one new person became a billionaire. (Peterson-Withorn, 2021)

Gain and loss have been unequally distributed across the winners and losers of this pandemic.

"The economic impact has been this extremely uneven thing where […] many hundreds of thousands or millions of small businesses have been hurt in a terrible way, but most of the big companies have overwhelmingly done fine," Warren Buffett observed.

Small businesses scrambled to keep the lights on. Families struggled to put food on the table. Meanwhile forty-five of the top fifty publicly traded companies in the United States turned a profit, according to the Washington Post. (Mac-Millan et al, 2020)

American automakers realized record profits by selling cars online before they arrived at the dealership. (Li, 2021) Amazon and Walmart collected an additional 10.7 billion dollars over 2019 profits, as consumers abruptly shifted from brick-and-mortar stores to online channels. (Kinder and Stateler, 2020) Pfizer raked in an astonishing 3.5 billion dollars of revenue in the first three months of 2021, from the production and distribution of the vaccines. (Robbins et al, 2021)

The fifty most valuable publicly traded organizations "collectively distributed more than $240 billion to shareholders through buybacks and dividends between April and September, representing about 79 percent of their total profits generated in that period." (MacMillian et al, 2020)

By December 2020 billionaire wealth ballooned at $11.95 trillion—for reference, that is equivalent to total COVID-19 recovery spending across the G20 governments. (Oxfam International, 2021) "Together, these Big Tech billionaires could end global hunger (for about $300 billion). Twice," Jane Chung, a Big Tech accountability advocate, wrote in a viral tweet. (McCarthy, 2021) She goes on to explain how billionaires in the Silicon Valley "could end global hunger, eradicate malaria, end homelessness in America, and end the famine in Yemen." (McCarthy, 2021) After doing this they would still have a measly twenty billion dollars to go around. (McCarthy, 2021)

American billionaires amassed enough money to pay for two-thirds of the COVID rescue package or provide a $3,900 check to every person in the United States. (Collins, 2021)

The government left this rent-seeking behavior unchecked as working-class Americans tightened their belts, put on their masks, and went to work. The working class risked their lives generating value that would never be returned to them.

Wealthy elites and large corporations hoarded their wealth, while the real winners of this pandemic rolled up their sleeves to combat these disproportionate outcomes.

Robert Smith, the wealthiest self-made Black man, rose to the occasion when he realized the government's Paycheck Protection Program marginalized Black businesses. The federal loan program distributed emergency relief payments to small businesses using an electronic system which very few Black businesses could access. (Lane, 2020)

"Seventy percent of African American neighborhoods don't have banks," Smith estimated. (Lane, 2020) Smith rose to action to combat this exclusionary banking. The software industry leader harnessed the power of his fintech company Finastra to develop a solution that paired Black small-business owners with financial institutions who had access to these federal loans. (Lane, 2020) He connected with the Conference of National Black Churches to let them know help was on the way. By May of 2020, the Finastra solution managed to pair ninety thousand Black entrepreneurs with loans to support both their businesses and their local economies. (Lane, 2020)

Melinda Gates vowed to accelerate recovery from the "she-cession" by donating $2.1 billion over the next five years to advance "women's economic empowerment, strengthen women and girls' health and family planning, and support women's leadership" amid the crisis. (Gates, 2021) Recovery efforts designed to address the needs of women would grow GDP by $13 trillion, according to a McKinsey & Company study.

Hans Vestberg, CEO of Verizon Communications, decided he would make every decision by considering his employees, customers, society, and shareholders—in that order. (Lane 2020) During the pandemic all 145,000 of his employees retained their jobs. (Lane, 2020) He vowed to continue providing service for customers regardless of their ability to pay. (Lane, 2020) "Verizon has provided every high school student in America with a *New York Times* subscription, handles connectivity and devices for kids at 350 schools and hosts free streaming 'Pay It Forward' concerts every week." (Lane, 2020)

The social services organization United Way opened Abilene United Way Camp in Texas to provide free day care for essential workers in need. The camp provides free lunches and enriching activities for the children thirteen hours a day as their parents work on the front lines of the crisis. (United Way)

The Abilene branch of the nonprofit also developed a volunteer driven Home Safe program, which "connects every single household in the community with a person in the same neighborhood to turn to for help." (United Way) The community powered network is supported by a suite of local assistance programs willing and able to step in as necessary. (United Way)

The Harlem Children's Zone, a global leader in antipoverty community-led initiatives, raised $26 million towards national COVID-19 relief and recovery efforts in 2020. (Harlem Children's Zone) To support Black communities disproportionately burdened by the negative economic, health, and social impacts of the virus, the Harlem Children's Zone plans to use this money to "inject vital resources into communities that have historically faced neglect and disinvestment." (Harlem Children's Zone) The nonprofit will partner with Black-led organizations to create a network of resources equipped to promote health care equality, social justice, and economic prosperity for the Black community nationwide.

This is a story of hope. A story of resilience, of triumph, and of defiance.

As we emerge from this pandemic our focus must be on reconstruction, not recovery. Recovery implies we return to the status quo. Reconstruction demands we leave normal behind and never turn back. It is up to us to know the difference.

We play a role in designing our future. I challenge you to adopt radical empathy, disrupt for inclusion, and design for equity every single day.

Radical empathy is the first step towards reconstruction. For corporations this means considering how your customers engage with their environments and designing solutions that improve their lives. For individuals this means actively seeking opportunities to learn more about the lived experiences of your peers and asking what you can do to be a better neighbor.

We can then disrupt for inclusion. This requires acknowledging the systemic nature of inequality in our country and committing to act against these forces of injustice. You have to accept your complicity in perpetuating marginalization and make tangible changes to counteract systems of oppression.

This disruption will allow us to design for equity. Let me be clear—designing for equity does not always mean equal outcomes. To create a level playing field, we must acknowledge how our nation has hindered the mobility of marginalized people and communities and pay reparations to enable equitable outcomes. There are no trade-offs, no quick wins, and no hard decisions when designing for equity. We have to work together, all at once, to understand alternative perspectives, heal wounds, and catalyze change.

It took a crisis for us to face our past. Let's not wait for another crisis to determine our future.

ACKNOWLEDGEMENTS

—

Writing a book is easy. Your goal is to put words on a page. They don't have to be the right words. They don't have to be inspiring. They don't even have to be good. But you write. After weeks, or maybe months, you look back on all you accomplished, and you realize: you just wrote a really terrible first draft.

Editing a book is hard. Your editor reads your writing and, by the grace of God, sees your vision. She works with you day in and day out to weave a beautiful narrative out of that mediocre first draft and challenges you to push yourself to deliver a book that will impact your readers.

Designing a cover is hard. Despite the age-old adage, people *do* judge a book by its cover. These artists transform your text into compelling visuals to draw your readers in.

Supporting an author is hard. Let's face it—we are super flaky. Our lives are controlled by our deadlines, and you support us anyway. I am awed by your selflessness.

Thank you to the village that supported me and transformed that first draft.

To my developmental editor Patricia Giramma, thank you for the 8:00 a.m. calls every Wednesday. Thank you for inspiring me to write every week and for giving me the courage to submit my first draft manuscript.

To my manuscript review editor Pea Richelle White, thank you for helping me find my voice as a writer, for pushing me to lead with humanity, and for teaching me how to tell a compelling story responsibly. Your unwavering support during the highs and lows of the editing process is the reason this book crossed the finish line.

Thank you to Gjorgji Pejkovski, Nikola Tikoski, and the cover design team for designing a compelling cover that brought my words to life. Thank you to my layout editor, Mateusz Cichocz, who transformed my words into a book.

To Ethan Jeffrey Green—thank you for holding down the fort at home, reminding me to eat, and offering words of encouragement when it felt like the world was caving in on me. When I told you I wanted to write a book you didn't laugh; you asked how we could make it happen. I love you and am endlessly humbled by how much you believe in me.

To my parents and biggest superfans—we did it! Thank you for cheering me on along the way and proudly sharing my campaign link with your friends.

Of course, I want to thank Dr. Robert Patterson, Sana Altaf, and Maggie Kervick for agreeing to be interviewed for the book. Your unique perspectives edified my knowledge on the material and added context and color to my writing.

To Eric Koester and the team at New Degree Press, thank you for taking a chance on me—for saying yes and providing the blueprint to make my dream a reality. Thank you for this platform. It has been an absolute privilege.

To those who preordered the book and shared my campaign site, thank you for investing in me. I am humbled by your generosity and honored to share this story with you.

Aaron Sun	Daniela Enright
Alan Moore	Daniela John
Alexandria Nelson	David Nichols
Allegra Bianchini	Debbie Warren
Angela Christie	Deborah Byers
Angela Estes	Devin Johnson
Anil Chitrapu	Diane Terrell
Anna Van der Linden	Donna Holt
Anthony Washington	Dylan Howlett
Avery Wine	Dylan Hunt
Caitlin Metcalfe	Dyllan Taxman
Carter McClain	Elena Snow
Cassie Ocilka	Emily Ettinger
Colleen McCarthy	Emily Huot
Colleen Sheridan	Eric Koester
Connor Ferraro	Erica Perlmutter
Cynithea Reeder	Erin O'Reilly
Daniel Clayton	Ethan Green

George Holt
Giana DiPasqua
Grace Berkman
Grace Kim
Gwendolyn Reilly
Hamilton Jenkins
Harneet Kaur
Hassan Shaikh
Jacin Fitzgerald
Jane Liu
Janice Lee
Jason Johnson
Jason Kanoff
Jenny McCracken
John Ackerman
John Enright
Jordan Curry
Jordan Portner
Juliana Molano
Kathryn Upton
Kaylan Coke
Kelli Austin Clarkson
Kellie Todoroff
Kelsey Read
Klaudia Konopka
Kristina Pham
Kristy Falango
Krystal Reddick
Lee Henderson
Les Bethune
Leslie Nelson
Leslie Patterson

Lincoln Lamberton
Lisa Read
Lizzie Berkovitz
Lola Faleti
Malcomb Coley
Mansi Vohra
Marcus Odedina
Maria Green
Mark Hawn
Marlena Konopka
Mason Hill
Matt Pinto
Matthew Williams
Michelle Darko
Michelle Nelson
Nicole Felix
Nicholas Molayem
Nicolle Holt
Noreen Metcalfe
Nwakaego Uzoh
Olivia Carmen Green
Patrick W. Lafferty
Peter McDonald
Pieter Melotte
Rachael Abt
Robbie Harms
Samuel Johnson
Samuel Yang
Sana Altaf
Sean Rhinehart
Shanterrie Martin
Shelby Dyl

Shirley Li
Stefanie Johnson
Susan Carpenito
Suzanne Trivette
Tatiana Shashou
Timothy Corcoran

Tina Cheesman
T.J. Nelson
Trish Kovach
Valerie Reilly
Zana Salzman

APPENDIX

INTRODUCTION

Baldwin, James. "As Much Truth as One Can Bear." *The New York Times*, January 14, 1962. https://timesmachine.nytimes.com/timesmachine/1962/01/14/118438007.pdf?pdf_redirect=true&ip=0.

Buchanan, Larry, Quoctrung Bui, and Jugal K. Patel. "Black Lives Matter May Be the Largest Movement in U.S. History." *The New York Times*, July 3, 2020. https://www.nytimes.com/interactive/2020/07/03/us/george-floyd-protests-crowd-size.html.

CDC Foundation. "What is Public Health?" Accessed December, 22 2020. https://www.cdcfoundation.org/what-public-health.

Centers for Medicare & Medicaid Services, Office of the Actuary, National Health Statistics Group. "The Nation's Health Dollar ($3.8 Trillion), Calendar Year 2019: Where It Came From." Accessed December 22, 2020. https://www.cms.gov/files/document/nations-health-dollar-where-it-came-where-it-went.pdf.

Georgiou, Aristos. "Pfizer COVID Shot Is Fastest Ever Vaccine to Be Approved in the West, First Licensed mRNA Jab in History." *Newsweek,* December 2, 2020. https://www.newsweek.com/pfizer-covid-west-mrna-1551754.

Harcourt, Jennifer, Azaibi Tamin, Xiaoyan Lu, Shifaq Kamili, Senthil K. Sakthivel, Janna Murray, Krista Queen, Ying Tao, Clinton R. Paden, Jing Zhang, Yan Li, Anna Uehara, Haibin Wang, Cynthia Goldsmith, Hannah A. Bullock, Lijuan Wang, Brett Whitaker, Brian Lynch, Rashi Gautam, Craig Schindewolf, Kumari G. Lokugamage, Dionna Scharton, Jessica A. Plante, Divya Mirchandani, Steven G. Widen, Krishna Narayanan, Shinji Makino, Thomas G. Ksiazek, Kenneth S. Plante, Scott C. Weaver, Stephen Lindstrom, Suxiang Tong, Vineet D. Menachery, and Natalie J. Thornburg. "Severe Acute Respiratory Syndrome Coronavirus 2 from Patient with Coronavirus Disease, United States." *Emerging Infectious Diseases Journal* 26, no. 6 (June 2020): 12661273. https://wwwnc.cdc.gov/eid/article/26/6/20-0516_article.

Haseltine, William. "Underfunding Public Health Harms Americans Beyond COVID-19." *Forbes,* October, 21 2020. https://www.forbes.com/sites/williamhaseltine/2020/10/21/underfunding-public-health-harms-americans-beyond-covid-19/?sh=22ee427e419c.

John Hopkins Bloomberg School of Public Health. "U.S. Health Care Spending Highest Among Developed Countries." Accessed December 22, 2020. https://www.jhsph.edu/news/news-releases/2019/us-health-care-spending-highest-among-developed-countries.html#:~:text=The%20researchers%20 determined%20that%20the,prices%20for%20many%20medical%20services.

Kearney, Audrey, and Cailey Muñana. "Taking Stock of Essential Workers." *KFF,* May 1, 2020. https://www.kff.org/policy-watch/taking-stock-of-essential-workers/.

LaBerge, Laura, Clayton O'Toole, Jeremy Schneider, and Kate Smaje. "How COVID-19 has pushed companies over the technology tipping point—and transformed business forever." *McKinsey & Company,* October 5, 2020. https://www.mckinsey.com/business-functions/strategy-and-corporate-finance/our-insights/how-covid-19-has-pushed-companies-over-the-technology-tipping-point-and-transformed-business-forever.

Maani, Nason, and Sandro Galea. "COVID-19 and Underinvestment in the Public Health Infrastructure of the United States." *Milbank Quarterly,* June, 2020. https://www.milbank.org/quarterly/articles/covid-19-and-underinvestment-in-the-public-health-infrastructure-of-the-united-states/.

McKillop, Matt, and Vinu Ilakkuvan. "The Impact of Chronic Underfunding on America's Public Health System: Trends, Risks, and Recommendations." *Trust for America's Health,* April, 2019. https://www.tfah.org/wp-content/uploads/2020/03/TFAH_2019_PublicHealthFunding_07.pdf.

New York Times. "Coronavirus World Map: Tracking the Global Outbreak." Last updated June 21, 2021. Accessed June 21, 2021. https://www.nytimes.com/interactive/2021/world/covid-cases.html.

Pramuk, Jacob. "Read Joe Biden's full 2020 Democratic National Convention speech." *CNBC,* August 21, 2020. https://www. cnbc.com/2020/08/21/joe-biden-dnc-speech-transcript.html.

Schaul, Kevin, Kate Rabinowitz, and Ted Mellnik. "2020 turnout is the highest in over a century." *The Washington Post,* November 5, 2020. https://www.washingtonpost.com/graphics/2020/ elections/voter-turnout/.

Tikkanen, Roosa, and Melinda K. Abrams. "U.S. Health Care from a Global Perspective, 2019: Higher Spending, Worse Outcomes?" *The Commonwealth Fund,* January 30, 2020. https:// www.commonwealthfund.org/publications/issue-briefs/2020/ jan/us-health-care-global-perspective-2019#:~:text=The%20 U.S.%20spends%20more%20on%20health%20care%20as%20 a%20share,higher%20than%20the%20OECD%20average.

Villeneuve, Denis, director. 2013. *Enemy,* Rhombus Media, E1 Entertainment, Pathé.

Yong, Ed. "How the Pandemic Defeated America". *The Atlantic,* September 2020. https://www.theatlantic.com/magazine/ archive/2020/09/coronavirus-american-failure/614191/.

CHAPTER 1 - DON'T FALL OFF THE CLIFF

Centers for Disease Control and Prevention. "About Chronic Diseases." Accessed January 16, 2020. https://www.cdc.gov/ chronicdisease/about/index.htm#:~:text=Chronic%20diseases%20are%20defined%20broadly,disability%20in%20 the%20United%20States.

Centers for Medicare & Medicaid Services, Office of the Actuary, National Health Statistics Group. "The Nation's Health Dollar ($3.8 Trillion), Calendar Year 2019: Where It Came From." Accessed December 22, 2020. https://www.cms.gov/files/document/nations-health-dollar-where-it-came-where-it-went.pdf.

Cutler, David, and Lawrence H. Summers. "The COVID-19 Pandemic and the $16 Trillion Virus." *Jama Network,* October 12, 2020. https://jamanetwork.com/journals/jama/fullarticle/2771764.

DocFleaPhD. "Cliff Analogy of Health." October 19, 2017. Video: 14:55. https://www.youtube.com/watch?v=2zAol4eKdFo.

Haseltine, William. "How US Public Health Failed You and Me." *Forbes,* October, 14 2020. https://www.forbes.com/sites/williamhaseltine/2020/10/21/underfunding-public-health-harms-americans-beyond-covid-19/?sh=22ee427e419c.

Haseltine, William. "Underfunding Public Health Harms Americans Beyond COVID-19." *Forbes,* October 21, 2020. https:// www.forbes.com/sites/williamhaseltine/2020/10/21/underfunding-public-health-harms-americans-beyond-covid-19/?sh=22ee427e419c.

John Hopkins Bloomberg School of Public Health. "U.S. Health Care Spending Highest Among Developed Countries." Accessed December 22, 2020. https://www.jhsph.edu/news/news-releases/2019/us-health-care-spending-highest-among-developed-countries.html#:~:text=The%20researchers%20determined%20that%20othe,prices%20for%20many%20medical%20services.

Kearney, Audrey, and Cailey Muñana. "Taking Stock of Essential Workers." *KFF*, May 1, 2020. https://www.kff.org/policy-watch/taking-stock-of-essential-workers/.

Kinder, Molly, Laura Stateler, and Julia Du. "The COVID-19 hazard continues, but the hazard pay does not: Why America's essential workers need a raise." *Brookings,* October 29, 2020. https://www.brookings.edu/research/the-covid-19-hazard-continues-but-the-hazard-pay-does-not-why-americas-frontline-workers-need-a-raise/.

Maani, Nason, and Sandro Galea. "COVID-19 and Underinvestment in the Public Health Infrastructure of the United States." *Milbank Quarterly* 98, no. 2 (June 2020): 250259. https://www.milbank.org/quarterly/articles/covid-19-and-underinvestment-in-the-public-health-infrastructure-of-the-united-states/.

McKillop, Matt, and Vinu Ilakkuvan. "The Impact of Chronic Underfunding on America's Public Health System: Trends, Risks, and Recommendations." *Trust for America's Health,* April, 2019. https://www.tfah.org/wp-content/uploads/2020/03/TFAH_2019_PublicHealthFunding_07.pdf.

Neilson, Susie and Yuqing Liu. "A timeline of Trump's statements about the coronavirus juxtaposed with new cases throughout the pandemic." *Insider,* October 27, 2020. https://www.businessinsider.com/what-trump-said-about-coronavirus-juxtaposed-case-count-2020-10.

Newsroom. "Chronic Disease, Poor Public Response Fuels COVID-19." October 16, 2020. https://newsroom.uw.edu/news/chronic-disease-poor-public-response-fuels-covid-19.

Raths, David. "Ohio Pediatric Effort Wins Hearst Prize for Population Health." *Healthcare Innovation,* October 6, 2020. https://www.hcinnovationgroup.com/population-health-management/news/21157321/ohio-pediatric-effort-wins-hearst-prize-for-population-health.

Yong, Ed. "How the Pandemic Defeated America." *The Atlantic,* September 2020. https://www.theatlantic.com/magazine/archive/2020/09/coronavirus-american-failure/614191/.

CHAPTER 2 - VIRUS HUNTERS

bioMérieux Connection. "June Almeida & The Discovery of the First Human Coronavirus." August 27, 2020. https://www.biomerieuxconnection.com/2020/08/27/june-almeida-the-discovery-of-the-first-human-coronavirus/.

Broadbent, Lindsay. "Coronaviruses - a brief history." *The Conversation,* April 15, 2020. https://theconversation.com/coronaviruses-a-brief-history-135506.

Centers for Disease Control and Prevention. "People with Certain Medical Conditions." Updated May 13, 2021. https://www.cdc.gov/coronavirus/2019-ncov/need-extra-precautions/people-with-medical-conditions.html.

Fall, Ibrahima Socé. "What Is an Outbreak Response?" FutureLearn, February 9, 2021. https://www.futurelearn.com/info/courses/disease-outbreaks/0/steps/62635.

Future Learn. "Key Interventions in a Disease Outbreak Response." *London School of Hygiene & Tropical Medicine,* 2019. https://

www.futurelearn.com/info/courses/disease-outbreaks/0/
steps/62646.

Marks, Lara. "June Almeida, the Life and Work of an Immune
Electron Microscopy Pioneer Who Opened up a New Understanding of Viruses." WhatisBiotechnology.org, May 15, 2020.
https://www.whatisbiotechnology.org/index.php/people/sum-
mary/Almeida.

National Foundation for Infectious Diseases. "Coronaviruses."
Accessed February 9, 2021. https://www.nfid.org/infectious-
diseases/coronaviruses/.

Ramirez, Vanessa Bates. "What is Ro?" *Healthline,* April 20,
2020. https://www.healthline.com/health/r-nought-repro-
duction-number.

Rogers, Kaleigh. "Why Did the World Shut Down For COVID-19
But Not Ebola, SARS Or Swine Flu?" *FiveThirtyEight,* April 14,
2020. https://fivethirtyeight.com/features/why-did-the-world-
shut-down-for-covid-19-but-not-ebola-sars-or-swine-flu/.

Williams, Shawna. "A Brief History of Human Coronaviruses."
The Scientist, June 2, 2020. https://www.the-scientist.com/
news-opinion/a-brief-history-of-human-coronaviruses-67600.

World Health Organization. "Coronavirus." Accessed February
9, 2021. https://www.who.int/health-topics/coronavirus#tab=-
tab_1.

World Health Organization Regional Office For The Eastern Med-
iterranean. "Epidemic and pandemic-prone diseases." Updated

January, 2020. http://www.emro.who.int/pandemic-epidemic-diseases/mers-cov/mers-situation-update-january-2020.html.

World Health Organization. "Timeline: WHO's COVID-19 response." Accessed February 9, 2021. https://www.who.int/emergencies/diseases/novel-coronavirus-2019/interactive-timeline?gclid=CjoKCQiAx9mABhDoARIsAEfpavQAazQjc_drK-J5HUEMAoEJVNoGmpSSoSHdPGY-S24x8DNpGgr6X46saA-sU-EALw_wcB#event-7.

CHAPTER 3 - WE SHOULD LISTEN TO BILL

Alegado, Siegfred. "Coronavirus Pandemic Could Cost the World $4.1 Trillion." *Time*, April 3, 2020. https://time.com/5814933/coronavirus-pandemic-cost-4-trillion/.

Foreign Policy. "The COVID-19 Global Response Index." Last updated March 15, 2021. https://globalresponseindex.foreignpolicy.com/country/australia/.

Millman, Zosha. "Today in history: Seattle began constructing the only U.S. fallout shelter tucked in an interstate." *SeattlePI*, May 15, 2019. https://www.seattlepi.com/local/seattle-history/article/Seattle-nuclear-fallout-shelter-history-Ravenna-13844773.php.

Oxford University. "Conspiracy Beliefs Reduce the Following of Government Coronavirus Guidance." May 22, 2020. https://www.ox.ac.uk/news/2020-05-22-conspiracy-beliefs-reduces-following-government-coronavirus-guidance.

Siliezar, Juan. "Responding to this pandemic, preparing for the next." *The Harvard Gazette*, May 13, 2020. https://news.harvard.edu/gazette/story/2020/05/pardis-sabetis-work-on-infectious-disease-coronavirus/.

Stieg, Cory. "How this Canadian start-up spotted coronavirus before everyone else knew about it." *CNBC*, March 3, 2020. https://www.cnbc.com/2020/03/03/bluedot-used-artificial-intelligence-to-predict-coronavirus-spread.html.

TED. "Bill Gates: The Next Outbreak? We're Not Ready." March, 2015. Video, 8:24. https://www.ted.com/talks/bill_gates_the_next_outbreak_we_re_not_ready.

"The COVID-19 Global Response Index." Methodology–The COVID-19 Global Response Index. Foreign Policy. Accessed June 17, 2021. https://globalresponseindex.foreignpolicy.com/methodology/.

Veith, Thomas. "A Preliminary Sketch of Wallingford's History." *Seattle.gov*, 2005. https://www.seattle.gov/Documents/Departments/Neighborhoods/HistoricPreservation/HistoricResourcesSurvey/context-wallingford.pdf.

Yong, Ed. "How the Pandemic Defeated America." *The Atlantic*, September 2020. https://www.theatlantic.com/magazine/archive/2020/09/coronavirus-american-failure/614191/.

CHAPTER 4 - THE PANDEMIC SURVIVAL GUIDE

Bremmer, Ian. "The Best Global Responses to the COVID-19 Pandemic, 1 Year Later." *Time,* February 23, 2021. https://time.com/5851633/best-global-responses-covid-19/.

Foreign Policy. "The COVID-19 Global Response Index." Last updated March 15, 2021. https://globalresponseindex.foreignpolicy.com/country/australia/.

Hassounah, Marwah, Hafsa Raheel, and Mohammed Alhefzi. "Digital Response During the COVID-19 Pandemic in Saudi Arabia." *Journal of Medical Internet Research* 22, no. 9 (September 2020). https://www.ncbi.nlm.nih.gov/pmc/articles/PMC7473704/.

Leacock, Matt. *Pandemic.* Roseville, Minnesota: Z-Man Games, 2019.

Maizland, Lindsay and Claire Felter. "Comparing Six Health-Care Systems in a Pandemic." *Council on Foreign Relations,* April 15, 2020. https://www.cfr.org/backgrounder/comparing-six-health-care-systems-pandemic.

Partridge-Hicks, Sophie. "5 Countries That Are Getting COVID-19 Responses Right." *Global Citizen,* September 11, 2020. https://www.globalcitizen.org/en/content/countries-with-best-covid-responses/?template=next.

Peñaloza, Marisa. "New Zealand Declares Victory Over Coronavirus Again, Lifts Auckland Restrictions." *NPR,* October 7, 2020. https://www.npr.org/sections/coronavirus-live-updates/2020/10/07/921171807/new-zealand-declares-victory-over-coronavirus-again-lifts-auckland-restrictions.

Petesch, Carley. "African nations seek their own solutions in virus crisis." *AP News*, May 11, 2020. https://apnews.com/article/66e8d6229ce8cfa535c3db2e821e7753.

Scudellari, Megan. "How Iceland hammered COVID with science." *Nature*, November 25, 2020. Updated December 1, 2020. https://www.nature.com/articles/d41586-020-03284-3.

Shesgreen, Deirdre. "Senegal's quiet COVID success: Test results in 24 hours, temperature checks at every store, no fights over masks." *USA Today*, September 6, 2020. https://www.usatoday.com/story/news/world/2020/09/06/covid-19-why-senegal-outpacing-us-tackling-pandemic/5659696002/.

Soendergaard Larsen, Morten. "COVID-19 Has Crushed Everybody's Economy—Except for South Korea's." *Foreign Policy*, September 16, 2020. https://foreignpolicy.com/2020/09/16/coronavirus-covid-economic-impact-recession-south-korea-success/.

Taylor, Chloe. "How New Zealand's 'eliminate' strategy brought new coronavirus cases down to zero." *CNBC*, May 5, 2020. https://www.cnbc.com/2020/05/05/how-new-zealand-brought-new-coronavirus-cases-down-to-zero.html.

Vision 2030. *National Transformation Program*. 2021. https://www.vision2030.gov.sa/v2030/vrps/ntp/.

World Health Organization. "Origins of the 2014 Ebola epidemic." Accessed June 28, 2021. https://www.who.int/news-room/spotlight/one-year-into-the-ebola-epidemic/origins-of-the-2014-ebola-epidemic.

CHAPTER 5 - REMEMBER THEIR NAMES

Arora, Maneesh. "How the Coronavirus Pandemic Helped the Floyd Protests Become the Biggest in U.S. History." *The Washington Post,* August 5, 2020. https://www.washingtonpost.com/politics/2020/08/05/how-coronavirus-pandemic-helped-floyd-protests-become-biggest-us-history/.

Aviles, Gwen. "Police killings are the sixth leading cause of death among young men, study shows." *NBC News,* August 13, 2019. https://www.nbcnews.com/news/nbcblk/police-killings-are-sixth-leading-cause-death-among-young-men-n1041526.

Baradaran, Mehrsa. *The Color of Money: Black Banks and the Racial Wealth Gap.* Cambridge: Harvard University Press, 2017.

Black Lives Matter. "About." Accessed June 17, 2021. https://blacklivesmatter.com/about/.

Brown, DeNeen L. "40 acres and a mule: How the first reparations for slavery ended in betrayal." *The Washington Post,* April 15, 2021. https://www.washingtonpost.com/history/2021/04/15/40-acres-mule-slavery-reparations/.

Brown, Melissa and Rashawn Ray. "Breonna Taylor, police brutality, and the importance of #SayHerName." *Brookings,* September 25, 2020. https://www.brookings.edu/blog/how-we-rise/2020/09/25/breonna-taylor-police-brutality-and-the-importance-of-sayhername/.

Congressional Research Service. "Unemployment Rates During the COVID-19 Pandemic." Last updated June 15, 2021. https://fas.org/sgp/crs/misc/R46554.pdf.

Gross, Terry. "A 'Forgotten History' Of How The U.S. Government Segregated America." *NPR*, May 3, 2017. https://www.npr.org/2017/05/03/526655831/a-forgotten-history-of-how-the-u-s-government-segregated-america.

Hassett-Walker, Connie. "The Racist Roots of American Policing: From Slave Patrols to Traffic Stops." *The Conversation*. Last updated June 2, 2020. https://theconversation.com/the-racist-roots-of-american-policing-from-slave-patrols-to-traffic-stops-112816.

History. "Enlightenment." Last updated February 21, 2020. https://www.history.com/topics/british-history/enlightenment.

Lang, Cady. "President Trump Has Attacked Critical Race Theory. Here's What to Know About the Intellectual Movement." *Time*, September 29, 2020. https://time.com/5891138/critical-race-theory-explained/.

Memmott, Mark. "Obama: 'Trayvon Martin Could Have Been Me 35 Years Ago'." *NPR*, June 19, 2013. https://www.npr.org/sections/thetwo-way/2013/07/19/203660128/obama-trayvon-martin-could-have-been-me-35-years-ago.

Morse, Michelle, Amy Finnegan, Bram Wispelwey, and Chandra Ford. "Will COVID-19 Pave The Way For Progressive Social Policies? Insights from Critical Race Theory." *HealthAffairs,* July 2, 2020. https://www.healthaffairs.org/do/10.1377/hblog20200630.184036/full/.

North, Anna. "How Racist Policing Took Over American Cities, Explained By a Historian." *Vox,* June 6, 2020. https://www.vox.com/2020/6/6/21280643/police-brutality-violence-protests-racism-khalil-muhammad.

PBS. "Causes of the Civil War." Accessed June 17, 2020. https://www.pbs.org/opb/historydetectives/feature/causes-of-the-civil-war/.

Roediger, David R. "Historical Foundations of Race." *National Museum of African American History and Culture.* Accessed June 17, 2021. https://nmaahc.si.edu/learn/talking-about-race/topics/historical-foundations-race.

Schindler, Marc and Jeremy Kittredge. "A crisis within a crisis: Police killings of Black emerging adults." *Brookings,* December 2, 2020. https://www.brookings.edu/blog/how-we-rise/2020/-12/02/a-crisis-within-a-crisis-police-killings-of-black-emerging-adults/.

Williams, Hubert and Patrick V. Murphy. "The Evolving Strategy of Police: A Minority View." *U.S. Department of Justice Office of Justice Programs,* January 1990. https://www.ojp.gov/pdffiles1/nij/121019.pdf.

Woods, Hiatt. "How Billionaires Saw Their Net Worth Increase By Half a Trillion Dollars During the Pandemic." *Insider,* October 30, 2020. https://www.businessinsider.com/billionaires-net-worth-increases-coronavirus-pandemic-2020-7.

CHAPTER 6 - SUSTAIN THE MOMENTUM

Asante-Muhammad, Dedrick. "The Reagan Era:Turning Back Racial Equality Gains." *HuffPost,* March 11, 2013. Last updated May 11, 2013. https://www.huffpost.com/entry/the-reagan-era-turning-bac_b_2838625.

Collins, Sean. "The Financial Case For Defunding The Police." *Vox,* September 23, 2020. https://www.vox.com/the-highlight/21430892/defund-the-police-funding-abolish-george-floyd-breonna-taylor-daniel-prude.

Desilver, Drew. "Turnout soared in 2020 as nearly two-thirds of eligible U.S. voters cast ballots for president." *Pew Research Center,* January 28, 2021. https://www.pewresearch.org/fact-tank/2021/01/28/turnout-soared-in-2020-as-nearly-two-thirds-of-eligible-u-s-voters-cast-ballots-for-president/.

Guo, Jeff. "America's Tough Approach To Policing Black Communities Began As a Liberal Idea." *The Washington Post,* May 2, 2016. https://www.washingtonpost.com/news/wonk/wp/2016/05/02/americas-tough-approach-to-policing-black-communities-began-as-a-liberal-idea/.

Harlem Children's Zone. "Our Mission and Values." Accessed June 17, 2021. https://hcz.org/our-purpose/our-mission-values/.

Huizen, Jennifer. "COVID-19: Once Hospitalized, Black Patients Are Less Likely To Die." *Medical News Today,* December 9, 2020. https://www.medicalnewstoday.com/articles/covid-19-once-hospitalized-black-patients-are-less-likely-to-die.

Jagannathan, Meera. "Black People Are Up To 6 Times More Likely To Be Killed By Police, Harvard Study Says." *MarketWatch,* June 28, 2020. https://www.marketwatch.com/story/black-people-are-up-to-6-times-more-likely-to-be-killed-by-police-harvard-study-says-2020-06-26.

King, Maya. "How Stacey Abrams and Her Band of Believers Turned Georgia Blue." *Politico,* November 8, 2020. https://www.politico.com/news/2020/11/08/stacey-abrams-believers-georgia-blue-434985.

McCabe, Bret. "Does The Militarization of American Police Help Them Serve and Protect?" *Johns Hopkin Magazine,* Spring 2015. https://hub.jhu.edu/magazine/2015/spring/aclu-militarization-of-police/.

Schaul, Kevin, Kate Rabinowitz, and Ted Mellnik. "2020 Voter Turnout Is The Highest In Over a Century." *The Washington Post,* November 5, 2020. Last updated December 28, 2020. https://www.washingtonpost.com/graphics/2020/elections/voter-turnout/.

TED. "Kwame Owusu-Kesse: 5 Needs That Any COVID-19 Response Should Meet." June, 2020. Video, 6:27. https://www.ted.com/talks/kwame_owusu_kesse_5_needs_that_any_covid_19_response_should_meet?language=en.

CHAPTER 7 - SINK THE SHIPS

Bashir, Nada. "James Dyson Designed a New Ventilator In 10 Days. He's Making 15,000 For The Pandemic Fight." *CNN Business.* Last updated March 27, 2020. https://www.cnn.com/2020/03/26/tech/dyson-ventilators-coronavirus/index.html.

Cain, Áine. "Early Walmart Drone Program Pilots Will Deliver Groceries And COVID-19 Tests To Customers. Here's Everything You Need To Know About The Retailer's Delivery Trials." *Insider,* September 25, 2020. https://www.businessinsider.com/walmart-drone-delivery-partnerships-tom-ward-2020-9.

Charm, Tamara, Anne Grimmelt, Hyunjin Kim, Kelsey Robinson, Nancy Lu, Mayank, Mianne Ortega, Yvonne Staack, and Naomi Yamakawa. "Consumer Sentiment And Behavior Continue to Reflect The Uncertainty of the COVID-19 Crisis." *McKinsey & Company,* October 26, 2020. https://www.mckinsey.com/business-functions/marketing-and-sales/our-insights/a-global-view-of-how-consumer-behavior-is-changing-amid-covid-19.

History."Hernan Cortes." *History,* November 9, 2009. Last updated October 9, 2019. https://www.history.com/topics/exploration/hernan-cortes.

Kestenbaum, Richard. "LVMH Converting Its Perfume Factories To Make Hand Sanitizer." *Forbes,* March 15, 2020. https://www.forbes.com/sites/richardkestenbaum/2020/03/15/lvmh-converting-its-perfume-factories-to-make-hand-sanitizer/?sh=-74577c734a9a.

LaBerge, Laura, Clayton O'Toole, Jeremy Schneider, and Kate Smaje. "How COVID-19 Has Pushed Companies Over The Technology

Tipping Point — And Transformed Business Forever." *McKinsey & Company*, October 5, 2020. https://www.mckinsey. com/business-functions/strategy-and-corporate-finance/ our-insights/how-covid-19-has-pushed-companies-over-the-technology-tipping-point-and-transformed-business-forever.

Lebowitz, Shana. "10 Books Every First-Time Manager Should Read." *Business Insider*, January 29, 2016. https://www.inc.com/ business-insider/books-new-managers-should-read.html.

Reeves, Martin, Lars Faeste, Cinthia Chen, Philipp Carlsson-Szlezak, and Kevin Whitaker. "How Chinese Companies Have Responded to Coronavirus." *Harvard Business Review*, March 10, 2020. https://hbr.org/2020/03/how-chinese-companies-have-responded-to-coronavirus.

CHAPTER 8 - WE CAN'T STOP THE CLOCK

Borunda, Alejandra. "Climate Change Is Roasting The Himalaya Region, Threatening Millions." *National Geographic*, February 4, 2019. https://www.nationalgeographic.com/environment/ article/himalaya-mountain-climate-change-report.

"Causes of Drought: What's the Climate Connection?" Union of Concerned Scientists. Union of Concerned Scientists, April 10, 2014. https://www.ucsusa.org/resources/drought-and-climate-change#:~:text=Global%20climate%20change%20affects%20 a,and%20increased%20evaporation%20and%20transpiration.

Climate Reality. "Climate Health Connection Infectious Disease." May 30, 2019. Video, 2:27. https://www.youtube.com/ watch?v=KbFbjqX5Ooc.

Climate Reality Project. "Dr. Michael Mann On Extreme Weather: We Predicted This Long Ago." October 21, 2017. Accessed June 17, 2021. https://www.climaterealityproject.org/blog/dr-michael-mann-extreme-weather-we-predicted-long-ago?_ga=2.77537429.1862974541.1613863799-623549638.1613863799.

Climate Reality Project. "Why Is 1.5 Degrees The Danger Line For Global Warming?" March 18, 2019. Accessed June 17, 2021. https://www.climaterealityproject.org/blog/why-15-degrees-danger-line-global-warming.

Climate Reality. "The Human Impact of Climate Change: Personal Stories from Bangladesh, India, and China." October 23, 2013. Video, 6:47. https://www.youtube.com/watch?v=uZYHA5_FTmI&t=9s.

Climate Reality. "The Human Impact of Climate Change: Personal Stories from Somalia, Ghana, and Kenya." October 23, 2013. Video, 7:55. https://www.youtube.com/watch?v=Bg9GXLoLpiQ.

Climate Reality. "The Human Impact of Climate Change: Personal Stories from U.S. and Mexico." October 23, 2013. Video, 7:52. https://www.youtube.com/watch?v=EyPl6S6Aqxo&t=5s.

Deam, Jenny. "A Year After Waldo Canyon Fire, Colorado Town Contends With Flooding." Los Angeles Times, August, 29, 2013. https://www.latimes.com/nation/la-xpm-2013-aug-29-la-na-manitou-springs-20130830-story.html.

Denchak, Melissa. "Are the Effects of Global Warming Really that Bad?" NRDC, March 15, 2016. https://www.nrdc.org/stories/are-effects-global-warming-really-bad.

Denchak, Melissa. "Fossil Fuels: The Dirty Facts." *NRDC*, June 29, 2018. https://www.nrdc.org/stories/fossil-fuels-dirty-facts.

DiChristopher, Tom. "Climate disasters cost the world $650 billion over 3 years—Americans are bearing the brunt: Morgan Stanley." *CNBC*, February 14, 2019. https://www.cnbc.com/2019/02/14/climate-disasters-cost-650-billion-over-3-years-morgan-stanley.html.

Erdman, Jeremy. "We Produce Enough Food To Feed 10 Billion People. So Why Does Hunger Still Exist?" Medium, Feb 1, 2018. https://medium.com/@jeremyerdman/we-produce-enough-food-to-feed-10-billion-people-so-why-does-hunger-still-exist-8086d2657539.

Figueres, Christiana and Tom Rivett-Carnac. "What the World Will Look Like in 2050 If We Don't Cut Carbon Emissions in Half." *Time*, April 22, 2020. https://time.com/5824295/climate-change-future-possibilities/.

Fountain, Henry. "How Bad Is Climate Change Now?" *The New York Times*, April 20, 2020. https://www.nytimes.com/interactive/2020/04/19/climate/climate-crash-course-1.html.

Hiley, Scott. "Myths of Capitalistm: The Myth of Scarcity." *People's World*, August 14, 2014. https://www.peoplesworld.org/article/myths-of-capitalism-the-myth-of-scarcity/.

Masson-Delmotte, V., P. Zhai, H.-O. Pörtner, D. Roberts, J. Skea, P.R. Shukla, A. Pirani, W. Moufouma-Okia, C. Péan, R. Pidcock, S. Connors, J.B.R. Matthews, Y. Chen, X. Zhou, M.I. Gomis, E. Lonnoy, T. Maycock, M. Tignor, and T. Waterfield (eds.). *Special Report: Global Warming of 1.5°C Summary for Policymakers.* IPCC, 2018. https://www.ipcc.ch/sr15/chapter/spm/.

Mbow, Cheikh, Rosenzweig, Cynthia, Barioni, Luis Gustavo, Benton, Tim, Herrero, Mario, Krishnapillai, Murukesan, Liwenga, Emma, Pradhan, Prajal, Rivera-Ferre, Marta. *Special Report on Climate Change and Land: Food Security.* IPCC, 2019. https://www.ipcc.ch/srccl/chapter/chapter-5/.

McFall-Johnsen, Morgan. "Painfully Slow Hurricanes, Deadly Heat, and Cities Without Water: What the Climate Crisis Will Look Like In the Next 10 Years, According To Experts." *Insider,* November 22, 2019. https://www.businessinsider.com/climate-change-in-the-next-decade-2019-11.

Mouginot, Jérémie, Eric Rignot, Anders A. Bjørk, Michiel van den Broeke, Romain Millan, Mathieu Morlighem, Brice Noël, Bernd Scheuchl, and Michael Wood. "Forty-Six Years of Greenland Ice Sheet Mass Balance From 1972 to 2018." PNAS. National Academy of Sciences, May 7, 2019. https://www.pnas.org/content/116/19/9239.

Ndlovu, Lungelo. "Heatwave Threatens To Slash Harvests In Drought-hit Zimbabwe." *Reuters,* March 12, 2019. https://news.yahoo.com/heatwave-threatens-slash-harvests-drought-091327032.html.

Rogelj, J., D. Shindell, K. Jiang, S. Fifita, P. Forster, V. Ginzburg, C. Handa, H. Kheshgi, S. Kobayashi, E. Kriegler, L. Mundaca, R. Séférian, and M.V. Vilariño

Special Report: Global Warming of 1.5°C Mitigation pathways compatible with 1.5°C in the context of sustainable development. IPCC, 2018. https://www.ipcc.ch/sr15/chapter/chapter-2/.

Smithsonian. "What Are Fossil Fuels?" Accessed July 3, 2021. https://ocean.si.edu/conservation/gulf-oil-spill/what-are-fossil-fuels.

"The Climate Clock." ClimateClock.World. Accessed June 18, 2021. https://climateclock.world/.

United Nations. "The Paris Agreement." Accessed June 17, 2021. https://unfccc.int/process-and-meetings/the-paris-agreement/the-paris-agreement.

"What Are Fossil Fuels?" Smithsonian, March 26, 2020. https://ocean.si.edu/conservation/gulf-oil-spill/what-are-fossil-fuels.

CHAPTER 9 - FLIP THE SCRIPT

Baradaran, Mehrsa. *The Color of Money: Black Banks and the Racial Wealth Gap.* Cambridge: Harvard University Press, 2017.

CNN. "Pelosi: Democrats are capitalists" February 1, 2017. Video, 2:57. https://www.youtube.com/watch?v=MR65ZhO6LGA.

Fernando, Jason. "Gross Domestic Product (GDP)." *Investopedia.* Last updated April 25, 2021. https://www.investopedia.com/terms/g/gdp.asp.

"Here's Everything the Federal Government Has Done to Respond to the Coronavirus So Far." *Fiscal Blog (blog).* March 15, 2021.

https://www.pgpf.org/blog/2021/03/heres-everything-congress-has-done-to-respond-to-the-coronavirus-so-far.

Jahan, Sarwat and Ahmed Saber Mahmud. "What is Capitalism." *International Monetary Fund,* June, 2015. https://www.imf.org/external/pubs/ft/fandd/2015/06/basics.htm.

Kapoor, Amit and Bibek Debroy. "GDP Is Not a Measure of Human Well-Being." *Harvard Business Review,* October 4, 2019. https://hbr.org/2019/10/gdp-is-not-a-measure-of-human-well-being.

Manchester, Julia. "Majority of young adults in US hold negative view of capitalism: poll." *The Hill,* June 28, 2021. https://thehill.com/homenews/campaign/560493-majority-of-young-adults-in-us-hold-negative-view-of-capitalism-poll.

Mutikani, Lucia. "COVID-19 savages U.S. economy, 2020 performance worst in 74 years." *Reuters,* January 28, 2021. https://www.reuters.com/article/us-usa-economy/covid-19-savages-u-s-economy-2020-performance-worst-in-74-years-idUSKB-N29X0I8.

Patton, Mike. "The Impact Of Covid-19 On U.S. Economy And Financial Markets." *Forbes,* October 12, 2020. https://www.forbes.com/sites/mikepatton/2020/10/12/the-impact-of-covid-19-on-us-economy-and-financial-markets/?sh=7c14c6b82d20.

Sainato, Michael. "Nancy Pelosi Embarrasses Democrats With Tone-Deaf Town Hall Appearance." *Observer,* February 2, 2017. https://observer.com/2017/02/nancy-pelosi-cnn-town-hall-appearance/.

Seipel, Brooke. "Pelosi town hall question on capitalism wasn't planned: report." *The Hill*, February 2, 2017. https://thehill.com/blogs/blog-briefing-room/news/317639-pelosi-town-hall-question-on-capitalism-wasnt-planned-report?rl=1.

Ted. "Mariana Mazzucato: What Is Economic Value, And Who Creates It." July, 2019. Video, 18:46. https://www.ted.com/talks/bill_gates_the_next_outbreak_we_re_not_ready.

Ucl. "UCL – University College London." UCL Institute for Innovation and Public Purpose. Accessed June 18, 2021. https://www.ucl.ac.uk/bartlett/public-purpose/.

Zarroli, Jim. "$3.1 Trillion: Pandemic Spending Drives The Federal Budget Deficit To A Record." *NPR*, October 16, 2020. https://www.npr.org/sections/coronavirus-live-updates/2020/10/16/924582156/-3-1-trillion-pandemic-spending-drives-the-federal-budget-deficit-to-a-record.

CHAPTER 10 – IT TOOK A CRISIS

Allison, Theresa A., Anna Oh, and Krista L. Harrison. "Extreme Vulnerability of Home Care Workers During the COVID-19 Pandemic—A Call to Action." *Jama Network*, August 4, 2020. https://jamanetwork.com/journals/jamainternalmedicine/fullarticle/2769095.

Collins, Chuck. "Updates: Billionaire Wealth, U.S. Job Losses and Pandemic Profiteers." *Inequality.org,* April 15, 2021. https://inequality.org/great-divide/updates-billionaire-pandemic/.

Gates, Melinda. "With the economic recovery failing women, now is the time to act on gender equality." *Bill & Melinda Gates Foundation*, June 30, 2021. https://www.gatesfoundation.org/ideas/articles/women-economic-impact-COVID-19.

Hanks, Douglas, Charles Rabin, and Martin Vassolo. "Miami-Dade closing bars, restaurants, gyms. Statewide no groups larger than 10 on beaches." *Miami Herald*, March 17, 2020. https://www.miamiherald.com/news/coronavirus/article241262451.html.

Harlem Children's Zone. "HCZ Raises $26 Million Towards National COVID-19 Relief and Recovery Efforts: Selected as 2020 Audacious Project Grantee." Accessed July 3, 2021. https://hcz.org/press-releases/hcz-raises-26-million-towards-national-covid-19-relief-and-recovery-efforts-selected-as-2020-audacious-project-grantee/.

Kaplan, Juliana. "American billionaires added $1.62 trillion to their wealth over the last 13 months." *Business Insider*, April 15, 2021. https://www.businessinsider.com/american-billionaires-add-trillion-wealth-inequality-last-13-months-ips-2021-4.

Kinder, Molly and Laura Stateler. "Amazon and Walmart have raked in billions in additional profits during the pandemic, and shared almost none of it with their workers." *Brookings*, December 22, 2022. https://www.brookings.edu/blog/the-avenue/2020/12/22/amazon-and-walmart-have-raked-in-billions-in-additional-profits-during-the-pandemic-and-shared-almost-none-of-it-with-their-workers/.

Kinder, Molly, Laura Stateler, and Julia Du. "The COVID-19 hazard continues, but the hazard pay does not: Why America's essential workers need a raise." *Brookings,* October 29, 2020. https://www.brookings.edu/research/the-covid-19-hazard-continues-but-the-hazard-pay-does-not-why-americas-frontline-workers-need-a-raise/.

Lane, Randall. "Greater Capitalism: How the Pandemic Is Permanently Reshaping Our Economic System For the Better." *Forbes,* May 26, 2020. https://www.forbes.com/sites/randalllane/2020/05/26/greater-capitalism-how-the-pandemic-is-permanently-reshaping-our-economic-system-for-the-better/?sh=51b65bee71c1.

Li, Yun. "Warren Buffett says the pandemic has had an 'extremely uneven' impact and is not yet over." *CNBC,* June 29, 2021. https://www.cnbc.com/2021/06/29/warren-buffett-says-the-pandemic-has-had-an-extremely-uneven-impact-and-is-not-yet-over.html.

MacMillan, Douglas, Peter Whoriskey, and Jonathan O'Connell. "America's biggest companies are flourishing during the pandemic and putting thousands of people out of work." *The Washington Post,* December 16, 2020. https://www.washingtonpost.com/graphics/2020/business/50-biggest-companies-coronavirus-layoffs/.

McCarthy, Joe. "This Viral Tweet Thread Shows How the World's Billionaires Could Help End Extreme Poverty." *Global Citizen,* April 8, 2021. https://www.globalcitizen.org/en/content/viral-tweet-thread-forbes-billionaires-list/?template=next.

Miami Dade Matters. "Households/Income Data for County: Miami-Dade." Last updated January, 2021. http://www.miami-dadematters.org/demographicdata?id=414&sectionId=936.

Oxfam International. "Mega-rich recoup COVID-losses in record-time yet billions will live in poverty for at least a decade." January 25, 2021. https://www.oxfam.org/en/press-releases/mega-rich-recoup-covid-losses-record-time-yet-billions-will-live-poverty-least.

Peterson-Withorn, Chase. "Nearly 500 People Became Billionaires During The Pandemic Year." *Forbes,* April 6, 2021. https://www.forbes.com/sites/chasewithorn/2021/04/06/nearly-500-people-have-become-billionaires-during-the-pandemic-year/?sh=5bee854025c0.

Robbins, Rebecca and Peter Goodman. "Pfizer Reaps Hundreds of Millions in Profits From Covid Vaccine." *The New York Times,* May 4, 2021. https://www.nytimes.com/2021/05/04/business/pfizer-covid-vaccine-profits.html.

Tavernise, Sabrina, Audra D. S. Burch, Sarah Mervosh, and Campbell Robertson. "'We Have Lost It All': The Shock Felt by Millions of Unemployed Americans." *The New York Times,* March 27, 2020.https://www.nytimes.com/2020/03/27/us/coronavirus-unemployed.html.

United Way. "All over the world, United Way is connecting people to vital services and resources during the COVID-19 crisis." Accessed July 3, 2021. https://www.unitedway.org/recovery/COVID-19/local-impact-stories#.